inside
the
flame

"An autobiographical string of pearls—sixty-six episodes from an unusually rich life, flocked with micro details—visual, tactile, emotional. Each may be enjoyed individually like poetry. Extraordinary reading."

Ralph Abraham
Chaos, Gaia, Eros

"In brief, potent vignettes, Christina Waters celebrates the deeper meanings lurking beneath everyday experience, and through a collection of memories and suggested activities, invites us to reimagine our own lives."

Lisa Jensen
Alias Hook

"*Inside the Flame* is a textured, flavorful exploration of the over-looked beauty in the everyday. Waters reminds us how to open our senses to experience the world. She shows us that every act can be a form of meditation, from washing socks to kissing. Don't let the fun, short chapters fool you; her vision is transformative."

Thad Nodine
Touch and Go

"Waters' book is a vibrant reminder of how crucial it is to live with the seasons of nature and of our own lives. Her eye for the beauty of simplicity, of clarity in living is invigorating. Bravo!"

Nicole Paiement
Conductor, Opera Parallèle

inside
the
flame

inside
the
flame

the joy of treasuring
what you already have

christina waters

PARALLAX
PRESS

Berkeley, California

contents

PART TWO : how the world touches us

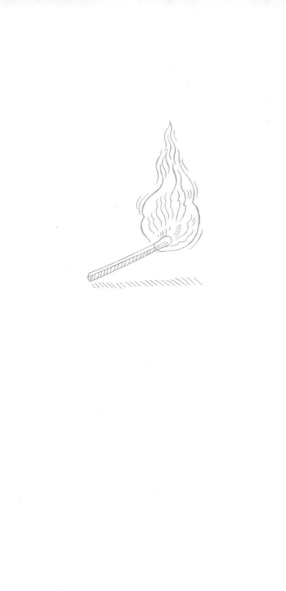

for Missy, companion of my childhood

Parallax Press
P.O. Box 7355
Berkeley, California 94707
parallax.org

Parallax Press is the publishing division of Unified Buddhist Church, Inc.
© 2016 by Christina Waters
All rights reserved
Printed in Canada

Cover and text design by Josh Michels
Illustrations © Alice Koswara
Cover image © Getty Images
Author photo © Shelby Graham
Illustrator photo © Eric Broers

[SFI logo]

Library of Congress Cataloging-in-Publication Data is available upon request.

ISBN: 978-1-941529-32-4

1 2 3 4 5 / 20 19 18 17 16

searching for home

For as long as I can remember, I have returned to the question: How can I feel at home in the world? As an Air Force brat, I had sixteen addresses before I left high school and twenty-one more after that.

Home was an elusive destination. Like the horizon, it was always receding, beyond reach no matter how fast I chased it. Because my family kept moving, home remained not only an elusive *somewhere* but also a perpetual *someday*. I longed to have a permanent place to which I belonged, and which would keep safe all my memories of family, friendship, and youthful discovery. For me it became romanticized into an image of a cozy house whose attic was filled with toys, scrapbooks, antique photographs, and outgrown clothes—the tangible perfume of holidays, birthdays, and rites of passage. Feeling at home became the goal of my life; it inspired everything I did.

With all that moving from place to place, I learned to act quickly to connect with people, to grow familiar with my surroundings, and to make friends. I wanted to feel, touch, sing, dance, love, explore, collect, drink, paint, walk, and see everything. Somewhere in all that active engagement I could surely find, or create, the place I sought. At some point I made the unconscious decision that survival meant embracing instability. Home would be wherever I happened to be.

I envied people whose houses had attics stuffed with childhood memorabilia. I gravitated toward friends with large, extended families, saying yes to dinner invitations whenever a grandmother might be at the table. Grandparents symbolized a warm, intimate connection with the past, especially a specific past of a specific family. I had known my own grandparents so briefly in the flurry of moving back and forth across countries and continents and had missed connecting through them to their own homes and origins. I missed being in touch with their rootedness in the era that had led to my own. I longed to ask an elder about her favorite memories, but by the time I reached out, the elders had slipped away. I acquired the sorts of rich, varied, and messy memories that only a wanderer can accumulate. Each encounter took the form of a question: Will this place, person, or act take root and sprout, grow tall and stay with me for the long run?

Perhaps because I had no roots to hold me tight to one path or one place, I was free to explore. In the process I have filled each event in my life with as much color, movement, and awareness as it could hold.

The quest for home has provided me with incredible joys, silly fun, and adventure as well as many awkward moments and occasional terrors. Along the way my attitude of curiosity helped to open doors, metaphorical as well as literal, which would otherwise have remained shut.

This book contains some tales of a life lived with all senses wide open. What follows is a close reading of the worlds contained in ordinary events, the eternities enmeshed in the body's enjoyment of the senses. Plunging into life with a sense of adventure has reinforced my capacity for excitement and heightened my sensitivity to everything I touch.

This is the story of my journey home.

how we touch the world

1

Reaching
and Holding

My earliest memory is of spinning around and around, dancing and laughing until my spinning grew so out of control that my tiny hand broke right through a window. I vividly recall being thrilled and shocked by the sound of breaking glass. I was two years old, we were living in Germany, and my parents had gone out to dinner leaving me in the care of a housekeeper. She must have rushed me to a doctor's office because by the time my parents returned home I had a huge bandage up to my right elbow. I remember my mother shrieking with alarm. But it was just a small cut on the hand. I still bear the scar and the juicy memory of how much fuss it all caused.

Try to recall your earliest awareness, the first thing you can remember. I'll bet it's about trying to reach out for something nearby, trying to hold on tight. For babies, this grasping is a reflex need to stay connected to the mother. Tiny fingers encircle the mother's single finger. Once reassured, the tiny hand begins to reach further. The desire to grasp the world is a question our body asks. What is out there? *Mother's hand.* And what else? What else is the world made of? The hands want more.

They seek information. Just how large is the world, what does it feel like?

Our hands are our oldest companions in the lifelong quest to learn the world. Our most intimate allies, our clever hands reach out to the world and bring it near. Hands love to hold just about anything. Mine get a kick out of wooden spoons, hammers, and ropes. These objects bring intriguing textures with them, as well as the opportunity to grip, to make a fist, to hold on tight. My hands have delighted in holding on to important parts of the natural world like trees, wildflowers, seashells, and rocks. They like to hold tight to other objects and vehicles that move me through the world in new ways.

My hands love the steering wheel of my car, the sense of power they feel when slowly turning the wheel wherever they decide to go. As a girl, my beloved turquoise Schwinn bicycle handles steered me along sidewalks, streets, and paths through the woods. Holding tight to wheelbarrow handles has let me move earth, rocks, leaves, and weeds in order to make a garden or to clean up after a storm. Holding the hand of someone I love, or of a struggling neighbor in need of help, or shaking the hand of someone I've just met and marveling at the simple magic of a hand-to-hand contact. Or course there's arm wrestling too, which the tomboy in me loved to play in grade school. Then there's holding tight but with some degree of tenderness to a guitar or a shared musical score.

My grandfather taught me to chop firewood into slender pieces of kindling. Patiently watching over me, he guided me through the steps of holding a piece of wood upright with one hand while carefully aiming a small axe into the end grain so that the wood would split neatly. The feel of the axe handle against my palm was instantly pleasurable, and the pride I took in watching a small stack of wood gradually build up rendered me pretty much speechless. I learned that my hands could transform mundane objects into something useful. I treasure both the lesson he gave me and the skill I acquired. Every outdoor barbeque is an excuse for me to show off my craftiness with a hand axe.

My hands also enjoy tasks using scissors, paintbrushes—especially watercolor brushes with their soft, eloquent bristles—and kitchen knives. Cutting carrots into tiny, diced cubes can be joyful for many senses at once: the eyes (they adore orange), the nose (sniffing the subtle, earthy sweetness of cut carrots), and the hands, having to be careful and clever about making those uniform and often exasperatingly difficult tiny shapes.

23

With practice comes increasing skill, like holding a racquet so it can neatly return the tennis ball or catching a fast-moving softball. Throwing a ball back and forth is easy fun that yields expertise, as you gradually learn exactly where the ball will be and placing your body in the right spot, catching the ball with your hand so that it doesn't drop.

Holding, grasping, the expertise of the hands, all begins with reaching outward. How much the world expands as we can reach further, higher. We use anything we can get our hands on: stools, steps, ladders. Improvising with tongs, sticks, poles. Standing on tiptoes, or on the shoulders of others. As our reach expands, so does the world.

2

Up High and
Down Low

As a kid, I needed to climb, the higher the better. Stairs, ladders, elevators, towers, trees, lighthouses, hills, and mountains all called to me, loudly. I would take every chance I got to get up higher than just standing or sitting would allow and crawled out onto more than one forbidden rooftop just to see what I could see.

Trees got my attention right from the beginning. Big and strong, loaded with scratchy branches and sweet fragrances, they seemed an obvious place to start testing how I fit into things. The minute I started climbing trees, my world got bigger. Who doesn't want to know whether the world can support her weight? The whole point of those early episodes of tree climbing—in addition to exhilaration—was to reach into the huge natural world. I wanted to get my little body into that tree.

That first handhold, finding the right branch, tests our strength to pull ourselves up. Once we do that, the trick is to find the next branch close enough to grasp. With a bit of agile squirming and twisting we manage to reposition our bodies so that we can, hopefully, pull ourselves up to the next accessible notch in the tree. We feel our muscles, our own strength in a whole new way. Tree climbing offers a chance to see a new view of the world, a world grown larger in a matter of minutes. Mountains appear in the distance that weren't there a moment before.

Trees give way to rooftops, rooftops reveal new features. I can remember the fabulous feeling of sitting in a tree, breaking free of the solid ground and suspending myself up high over people and cars and houses below.

Holding on involves balance, learning how to balance our bodies the right way so as not to fall. Our feet have to learn their role in tree climbing, they must find the next safe, strong platform. Even trickier is inching our way back down the tree, a journey in reverse. The same tree, yet the descent is entirely different. Going down requires a new set of skills and a different sort of courageous curiosity. Watch how easily a cat can jump and scamper up a tree, yet how skittishly and hesitantly it descends.

25

The whole point of holding tight to the tree's branches became abruptly clear to me when I fell out of a tree. I was about six years old. Since it wasn't a very big tree, I didn't fall more than seven feet before I landed on my back. What a shock. The most terrifying thing was that I couldn't breathe. I had fallen with such impact I had knocked the breath out of my lungs. But by the time my mother arrived, I had already struggled to my feet. Nothing was broken, just a few scrapes. But I had learned a lot about the dangers of not knowing my own limitations—and the vast scale of nature. I also learned you actually could survive some bumps and bruises and that you can only learn by making mistakes, ones as common and ordinary as failing to grip a branch tightly enough.

I still longed to be up high in that tree. I wasn't going to be denied the pleasure of climbing higher, and the next day I found the nerve to climb that tree again. This time I held on tight. I was rewarded with a confidence in my body's abilities and some outstanding views of the immediate world around our apartment on Andrews Air Force Base. Hard to imagine how much I would have missed if I had never tried climbing a tree again.

As an adult, I have climbed up to the towers and domes of monuments and cathedrals. I remember lugging a shopping bag from the Louvre Museum up the stone bell tower of Notre Dame

Cathedral, an arduous ascent of 300 steps that was quickly forgotten once I savored the view of the River Seine and all of Paris stretched out below. The cramped spiral staircase of Barnegat Lighthouse was worth a climb recently. I could watch New Jersey flatten and the Bay stretch as I climbed, until I emerged at the top into gale force winds and a sublime panorama of the Atlantic. Climbing to a perch at the top of *anything* has never let me down.

Looking out tiny windows every few steps, I watched the world below grow smaller. The air became bluer, distances receded, until emerging onto the rooftops I feasted on the sight of the town and countryside. Up high, I could trace rivers, examine the rooftops and the different styles of architecture. Fields, valleys, and forests acquired new magic as they became almost doll-like in their new miniature sizes. How all of these man-made and natural landmarks fit together made more sense to my eyes— the interweaving of everything I saw. I could see how far away the road was from the town. If the sky was clear, I could catch the sun glinting off the ocean on the far horizon. Here was a living map of a world I'd only known close up. And now it acquired new possibilities. I could take a certain road knowing that it would lead to the mountain. As my eye followed a road, and stayed with it as it turned and straightened, I could read how it had been laid down, the logic of its path. I could immediately grasp why it had to bend sideways because of the river and then straighten to go past the center of town. That knowledge was no longer something abstract, existing only in words or maps. It was now mine, known to my eyes and in my body.

The view from the top unfolds in so many ways. Even getting on a ladder in order to pick some fruit from the top of the tree lets you become another creature, a bird perhaps, and see how things are arranged below, rather than simply next to, your body. From above, the world appears to organize itself around my body at its center. It flows in every direction around me;

wherever I turn and look, there is more to see, more trees than I ever could have seen from ground level.

Seen from Below

Another way of understanding our bodies in relation to the size of the world is to crouch down on the ground and look up. As a kid, I would squeeze into caves, or burrow into culverts or storm drains, those corrugated aluminum tubes used to divert water away from streets. From there I felt like an unseen secret viewer—a hidden voyeur—as the world went about its business above me.

How exciting the world looked when viewed from below. All the more exciting since I was using secret eyes, and as I looked up at the world, it acquired a special sort of organization. Feet were large and close; heads were smaller and farther away. Those altered vantage points expanded my mind and body's notion of the world around me. Nothing, it turned out, was actually "ordinary" at all.

View from the cellar window: feet moving around in the garden; tall grass substantial as emerald forests; the neighbor's cat lying in wait, stalking some hapless bird, a bird simply going about its business unaware of the danger that I could see from my hidden vantage point. Weeds, logs, garbage cans, the neighbor's driveway across the street, all of it newly strange and focused like the iris lens on an old film camera. Standing on tiptoes, peeking out through the narrow cellar window, I was invisible and hence possessed the supernatural powers that accompany invisibility. I learned something about being still and watching, about how the world offers many views, depending upon where you sit, stand, jump, or lie.

The world is a varying multiplicity—it isn't just one thing after all, it is a multiverse. From all these different vantage points, the ecology of a place and its surroundings become something like visual music. I didn't yet know all the words but I could hum a few bars.

your turn

Give yourself some unknown views. Explore the highs and lows of your surroundings. Climb a tree. Check out an unknown stairway. Wade in a creek. Go up onto the roof of your house or apartment building and draw a map of your neighborhood.

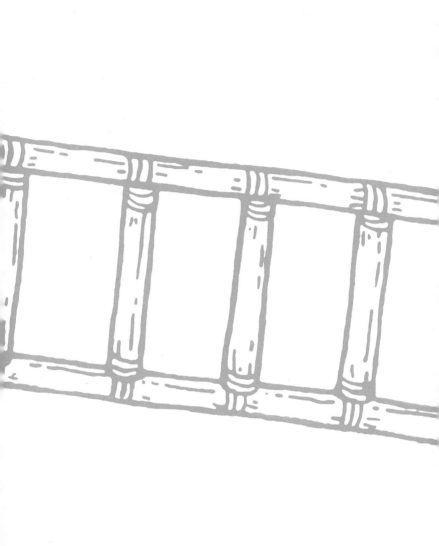

3

Daring to Move

"Come join us!" Jesse waved to me from across the room. My body couldn't resist. Flushed with spiced foods, wine, and the insistent rhythm of music, I rose without thinking and inserted myself into the spiral of dancers circling the hotel ballroom. Jesse was a talented cook with an abundant body and a wide-open smile. We had come to the island of Crete, with other chefs, writers, and anthropologists for a Mediterranean food conference. There she was, along with fifteen other women holding hands, feet skipping forward and back, moving in a deliberate circle to the hypnotic sounds of the Greek pipes and zither. I joined them, and as the circle spiraled around and around, our cheeks grew red, our smiles more dreamy, and we all slipped into another world. It was the same world those Minoan priestesses inhabited with snakes raised high. The movement of our bodies had sent us through a portal—we were transported—and we became a single dancer, eyes closed, inside a place both sacred and profane.

Then I heard the crashing of plates. It was unmistakable. Bodies still swaying and circling the floor, but now plates were crashing to the floor. This was not accidental breakage. Each dancer grabbed a plate from a pile on the banquet table and when the impulse claimed her, she would throw it to the floor, thrilled by the sonic vibration of the china smashing to pieces. They were all doing it! "It's traditional," someone whispered to me. I grabbed a plate, still dancing, and flung it to the floor in an act of abandon I'd never dared before.

Last spring I sat down in the meadow near my house. A small crowd of Monterey cypresses gathered behind me, and the grass I sat on seemed to tumble down into the blue-gray Pacific. No one was around, so I leaned forward, poised myself carefully, and pushed my body, head over heels, into a somersault. Nothing broke, so I did it again. It felt like instant childhood. My body smiled in recognition. When was the last time you lay on a hilltop and rolled down, just letting your body go rolling and rolling until you stopped? A long time ago, wasn't it? It's a simple recipe for feeling silly and excited and a tiny bit like you did when you were a kid. And what did I gain by rekindling that childhood feeling? The giddy sensation of sheer play for its own sake, for one thing, and the awareness of my body pushing against the ground in an unfamiliar motion (for most adults anyway) that shook up my ordinary ways of moving. I noticed all over again where my shoulder jutted out, where my stomach protected my body from the hard ground. I got in touch with gravity, with rarely used movements, feelings, and limitations. I felt a kind of physical freedom I had forgotten. It was still within reach.

I've been stopped in my tracks watching children in stores, wild with excitement over just how much they can see, how much they want to touch *anything* that attracts their attention. Seeing them is a reminder of my first ecstasies of reaching, touching, and moving through whatever's out there. Babies aren't even that discriminating—they take incalculable pleasure in discovering their own feet, objects that might as well be the family cat or a strange pink fruit.

I can recall the insane joy I felt in holding impromptu races with my playmates—let's see who can get to the stop sign first! Whether I won the race or not, I learned a bit more about what my legs, body, and muscles could do. Or couldn't do.

I constantly test the size and shape of the world by moving my body in all kinds of ways. As I experiment with moving, the world acquires new lightness or heaviness, resistance or ease. If riding a boogie board is a way of removing the resistance of the world, then running uphill is a quick way of discovering just how much of a fight the material world can put up. The sweat on my shoulders, my panting breath proves I've met a worthy opponent.

The variations are endless. I used to twirl until I fell down, laughing, head spinning. It was a game I played with girlfriends, a let's-test-our-limits game. It felt beautiful, the endless motion, the circular whoosh with my body at the very center. Remember twirling until you fell down dizzy?

Feet love to be bare so they can make personal probes and explore for fluctuations of temperature and texture. Running barefoot through grass still gives my feet a sensuous treat, and if the grass is wet with dew, so much the better. Feet love to squish and slide. Feet get excited by stomping. We understand our grounding in the world thanks to our feet. Feet are so easy. Just remove your shoes and see how happy they are. Running helps my feet learn how to reach further, climb higher, and ultimately look great in fashionable shoes.

Think of all the games children play that require sneaking, creeping, crawling, and slithering. They are how the body learns just how many secret ways and means it can access. And of course there's dancing, moving the body in precise—or improvised—ways to music. The dancing I loved most involved ritual movements that showed off the body's grace and strength, and most involved the joining of hands, the embrace of the entire body, touching to music. My feet can still feel the insistence of a country square dance reel, whirling around and around, only to be caught by the hands of another before whirling around again. Slow dancing gave me my first chance to learn the power of music to spark romance. Dancing with John Ryan in high school. The movements brought him close to me, in a way that was purely biological and completely exploratory. That first embrace with an attractive other—dancing provided just the excuse I needed to be close to another body. Animal attraction did the rest.

Extreme Play

I was not a quiet child. I liked to talk. I liked to sing. I liked attention. I was always pushing simple acts of play into huge events. High-spirited games resonated throughout my young world, if only for the duration of a scream.

My younger sister was always up for anything I suggested. We invented a game we called "Feet Fight," in which we lay on the floor with our feet touching. At my command we would bend our knees so that the soles of our feet rose up above our bodies, still touching. Once we were in position, one of us would yell, "Feet fight!" and our feet would begin fighting. It was blitheringly fun, silly, and often painful. We would kick at each other's feet until we were exhausted. Then we lay panting and laughing at the sheer silliness of our mock combat.

We never actually discussed the ground rules, or what we were going to do once our feet were touching and ready for action. It simply erupted from our shared sense of fun. The more our mother found it shocking and exasperating, the more we loved launching into an impromptu bout of fighting feet. We continued this little game of our own invention until I left for college.

When we play we're experimenting with what we want and how far we can push it. When playing "outside the lines," it's up to us to invent, discover, improvise. We're building a world we would like to see; a world we might like to inhabit. We experiment with the sizes, shapes, and colors of possible scenarios, and each scenario is connected to a world that we might, or might not, bring into existence. Through play we become who we might be, and we invite into existence (if only for as long as playtime lasts) a world we will love.

Play is a fortune-teller, foreseeing what we might be good at later on. Making up songs, playing at little dramas, making up dances—this sort of play might be a warm-up act for a life in performance. Are we fast? Running games help us to discover our abilities. Are we well coordinated? Trying a game of baseball, tennis, or soccer will give us a clue. Organizing games with lots of collaborators might be training us for a leadership role in adult life. Entertaining ourselves alone on a rainy day can build strategies for surviving, even enjoying solitary moments yet to come. Or playing may simply be a way of staving off full-blown adulthood for another few months.

There's structured play—games, sports, drama—each bordered by its own set of rules and conditions. There's free play, like Feet Fight. And there's a kind of play that falls somewhere in between the two, where you make up your own rules within some shared stories already running through the cultural environment. For example, let's play Robin Hood—I'll be Robin, you be the Sheriff of Nottingham. I loved organizing games, assigning roles for my friends to play. Then everybody had to go all out in creating characters. We'd make castles out of washing machine packing crates and rummage for possible costumes in our mother's laundry or among a father's threadbare work clothes.

We'd set up the plot for the day. The Sheriff has just taken away the villagers' entire harvest of potatoes and Robin and his Merry Men must rescue the harvest and return it safely to the villagers. Or bad guys are coming and we have to protect the castle. And off we'd go, across the frontage road that ran behind our apartment and into the trees. By the time we'd scrambled into the trees, they officially became Sherwood Forest for the day.

Another kind of play seems to pop up organically from a single moment of inspiration or purely by chance. You hear something silly on TV and you begin to mimic it. Pretty soon you start speaking in a ridiculous artificial accent and walking through the living room in an exaggerated fashion, repeating the infectious word. What you're doing is creating a magical space in which you (and your playmates, perhaps) are transformed into new beings. Voices change, bodies become stiff or rubbery, grotesque or hyperactive, and more often than not, extreme fits of the giggles take over as the action is pushed to its limits. And the play fractures into a thousand pins and needles of delight and exhaustion. The original inspiration, even though it was not even brought into consciousness, has played out its natural lifespan. You were its carrier, the vehicle in which it enjoyed its modest moment, and then dissolved. You were then released from its spell and turned back into a human girl or boy.

Nonsense play was a specialty at my house, where first one, then another, and finally all four of us would find ourselves around the piano howling nonsense songs, which led to my father grabbing his trumpet and joining in while we marched around the kitchen, dining room, and into the bedrooms, clowning, crooning, and erupting in unearthly and unscripted foolishness.

One of my favorite kinds of play that has absolutely no purpose except making toes curl with pleasure is playing in the snow. If there's snow around, I go wild with excitement. I can't resist touching it, forming it into balls, throwing it. The mineral electric purple aroma of fresh snow is an addictive sensation. Who can resist? No question about it, snow must be touched, shaped, wallowed in, eaten, stomped, and finally surrendered to. All children throw themselves into the snow, lying in its frozen creaminess for no reason except to be there, to share in its secret silence. This must be done swiftly since part of the pleasure of snow is that it will melt *soon*. It will not last. So we embrace it quickly the minute it comes down to us on earth.

Play has permeated my entire life way beyond childhood. Assigning dramatic parts for my friends to play gave me a sense of confidence and polished my leadership skills. Even now I give free rein to my sense of play pretty much every day. When my sweetie, Jack, and I say goodbye to each other in the morning, we engage in an elaborate little dance of blowing kisses and calling "Ciao, ciao!" to each other, as if we were a couple of Borgias bidding farewell in Renaissance Italy. "Ciao," I call as Jack pulls out of the driveway. "Ciao," he calls back to me. Again I respond, and he continues. "Ciao," we boldly cry, back and forth until we can no longer hear each other's voices. Neither of us knows how that ritual evolved, but it did. At the very least our high-spirited goodbye ritual amuses the neighbors. At best, it's a way of making love in public, reinforcing our childlike delight in being together. The older I get the more I wonder why adults don't revisit the fun of childhood play. By staying connected with my younger self, I have shaped a life in which I am never bored.

My father never picked up a newspaper without reading the comics. Can you enliven your adult days (or nights) with some advanced child's play? What's stopping you? Did you love a certain game when you were a kid? Invite a fellow adult to join you in a few rounds of play. Head for a playground and zoom down the slide. Don't forget to yell.

your
turn

Collecting

From my dining table I can see a windowsill full of objects collected from various corners of my life. They display themselves for my enjoyment, or nostalgia, or sheer visual dazzle. On the counter, arranged in no particular order, are a cast-iron door knocker from a Cairo bazaar, a resin pyramid containing Oaxacan love charms, an enamel box overflowing with leathery sharks' eggs gathered on a New Jersey beach, a massive magnolia seedpod sitting next to a clay statue of the Hindu goddess Kali, and Kali herself standing (with the help of a glob of putty) atop a mosaic globe from a now-defunct antique shop. A cluster of pink peppercorns from my mother's tree in San Diego nestles with a handful of shells and rocks in a Mexican pottery bowl that was a birthday present from a dear friend. A tiny headless bronze Buddha perches next to the smiling figure of Ganesh. And I have many such eclectic altars and shrines throughout my house. Come to think of it, I always have.

As the seasons change, so does the collection of treasures. A branch of holly shows up around Christmastime. At Easter, tiny chicks and rabbits made of pink and yellow feathers and ribbons congregate around painted Russian eggs. Miniature pumpkins enter the picture in October, and at any moment the odd rock, seashell, or redwood cone finds its way into the evolving array.

Holding down the center of my windowsill is an assemblage that most closely approximates the ordinary meaning of collection—objects grouped by a common theme. My grandmother collected S&H Green Stamps and Meissen milkmaids. My mother collects wasps' nests. I have managed to acquire an unlikely group of spheres: an ornament embedded with mirrors from an import store, two quartz globes from a gem show, a huge lead crystal orb large enough to support an embroidered fez. Smaller spheres surround these large ones: an alabaster sphere from a trip to Tuscany, a glass marble that belonged to my mother in her marble-shooting childhood, a lead fishing weight, a dried datura gourd, perfectly preserved, that came home with me from a trip to the Mojave. These rhyming shapes make a soothing meditation for the eyes and have staked out their territory in my dining room for over a decade.

41

My windowsill gallery may be personal, but it is not unique. It would be hard to find any human dwelling without its shelf, table, or countertop collection of objects special and particular to the inhabitants. This tendency to bring home eye-catching bits of the world is not merely a habit; I believe it is a human passion. We need to have certain mementos from the outside world around us. They reflect our joys, our memories, and our interests back to us, and are among the many mirrors formed by reaching out and examining our environments. In them we see ourselves. They create coziness, a feeling of belonging, often for little or no cost. And in almost all cases—exceptions such as Barbie dolls, model airplanes, and plastic trolls come to mind—they are highly personal and idiosyncratic. No one else has my windowsill array. Each object came into my habitat by my own hand. And each one of my shrines has its own personality.

Every child has the instinctive hankering to collect. Remember when you were a kid? Every day—every *thing*—was exciting.

You were smaller of course, and closer to the ground. But you touched the world in countless ways as you went through your days, feeling, tasting, grabbing, climbing. The world was fresh and vibrant, and you carried much of it home with you in your hands and your pockets.

Each of us can recall this need to bring home bits of the world and put them on our windowsills, our kitchen tables, or to give to our mothers or fathers. Special branches covered with moss and lichens, brilliant autumn leaves, bird skulls, rocks embedded with shimmering mica or pyrite, the odd stick, weed, or feather. All of these bits of childhood wanderings were brought home and formed those first collections that we loved and which have invariably, over the years, disappeared into the same mysterious somewhere as love letters and report cards from second grade.

Why are we especially drawn to certain objects? We love the way they look, their curious colors and shapes. But why do we pick them up? Why are we drawn to them? And why is collecting them—gathering them, bringing them home, arranging them for display or tucking them away in hidden, special places—why is this important?

The objects we keep around us speak to a deep inner core of our lives. As we touch them from time to time we expand. They become our surrogates or alter egos. If this sounds like magic, perhaps it is. Our relationships with everything, and with everyone around us, are rarely built upon rational choices or practical considerations. Usually impulse, intuition, and emotion are at work in our give and take with the world. There was no reason why I picked up just this rock on the beach. It called to me. My hand reached out. I immediately responded to the feel of it in my hand, as my fingers curled around the stone's surface worn smooth and tumbled by the surf. The rock responded by nestling into the palm of my hand, fitting it in a way that is both familiar and new. This rock will come home with me. I put it safely in my pocket and bring it home to live on my windowsill.

Such collected objects aren't simply isolated entities. They are portals through which their native habitat is brought closer. As I touch the rock again with my hands or even simply with my eyes, it is not just the piece of softly eroded stone I encounter—it is *that* beach, *that* day, the salt air, the sound of the gulls overhead, the rumble of waves, my sweetheart walking with me along the shore. That irreplaceable and unique moment endures within the rock I have collected. It and I now exist in unspoken agreement. From now on, we have penetrated each other's lives. The larger world has moved closer to me, and I in turn have agreed to protect this small object within my personal journey. The world and I—this sea-tossed rock and my hand—enrich each other. Through it, I care for the earth.

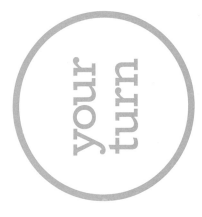

your
turn

Hold your favorite rock. Then close your eyes. Exhale and listen. Allow yourself to expect something unexpected. The rock has its own history. If you tune into it, you might find yourself involved in a new intimate alliance. What is its story? Listen, feel, and it will permeate your consciousness. So what if it sounds silly or weird. There's nothing to lose.

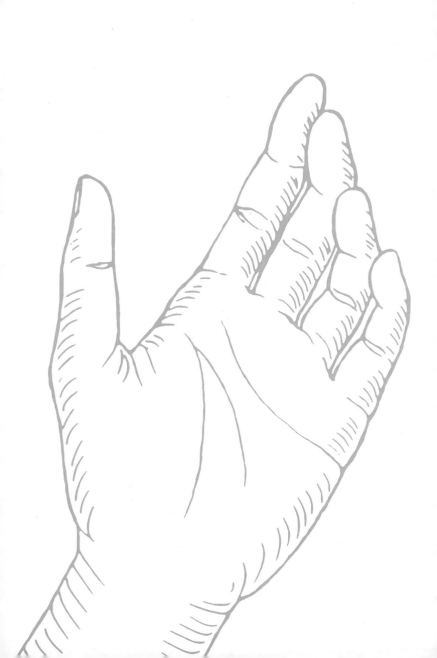

6

Petting Cats

Big, orange, and laid-back, Nicky introduced himself a few weeks after we'd moved into our house. Nicky was a special cat. He belonged to the neighbor whose garage adjoined ours. He was one of those very feline felines: completely free-range, a gifted predator, and a real lover.

My earliest memories of my grandfather involved going out into the backyard with him and helping him put out food for "the cats." Neighborhood strays, probably. I can still see his large, weathered hands, putting out old cracked bowls of cat food. A big yellow cat named Lucky was my grandpa's favorite. Sometimes, Lucky came into the house at night. He'd jump up onto the bed with me and curl up in the warm hollow made by my legs. The weight of him, the sound of his purring, made a deep and lasting impression on me.

As a big orange cat, Nicky was the embodiment of my childhood cat archetype. He would often come to the back of the house and sit with his nose pressing the glass of the sliding doors. He waited until we opened the doors, then he came in, walked to a spot in the center of the rug by the dining table, and sat down. Posing, making sure he was seen at his largest, his furriest, his best.

With luck, I could entice Nicky to come up onto my lap. In a bound, the void that is the air mass just above my thighs is filled—plop!—with another being, shaped and sized to the exact dimensions of a human lap. Once the heavy warmth of fur-encased flesh has found its niche on my lap, the trance state begins. His eyes begin to close. The purring starts. The sensation of the rising and falling of Nicky's breath was indescribably pleasurable. The feline body snatcher had temporarily appropriated me, the human subject. He was now taking over my will. Just try to get up once a cat has made itself comfortable on your body.

Nicky always responded to my touch with a purr. I cannot resist that seismic vibration, the low Russian chorus waves of voluptuous sound. Purring feels like an animal lullaby, a shamanic, trance-inducing rumble. Cat lovers I know will do almost anything to get a cat to that ecstatic state and then feast on the hypnotic sound.

Petting cats is a primal pleasure for the hands. Most of the time we look past the touch and its sensations and into the project we're undertaking. The body is quite often "invisible" in our day-to-day activities, overlooked in favor of the task. But if we switch the focus for a moment—think of this mental exercise as switching the lens on a microscope—we can savor the body's awareness of what it's doing. As you pet a cat, you can feel his pleasure, you can watch how much he is enjoying your touch. You can also move your attention to your hand itself, and the enormous soothing, vibrant sensation the hand is enjoying as it runs along the fur, feeling the living creature inside the fur, its beating heart and warmth. Cats are seductive bridges between the human and the mysterious. To touch Nicky was to be captured by the nonhuman in living, breathing, impossibly soft form. In him I had communion with another species that touched me back.

Another aspect of feline seduction involved the sensation of Nicky's paws pressing on my arm or leg. The paw that asks, insists, probes. Sometimes his paws became so overwhelmed with pleasure that his claws appeared. Abandon had taken over and he simply let go of his inhibitions. The claws and paws curl and release, curl and release in the throes of pleasure. I was necessary only to cooperate with his hedonistic needs. I must pet him. I must not move. I must allow him to walk on me, sit on me, lay upon me if he desired. I must allow him to have his way with me—to take me over.

The tongue is another attraction; the unique surface is part tickle, part moist caress. The tiny diagonal grooves on the tongue make rough traction with each lick. Fingers and hands continue tingling long after a cat tongue massage.

Nicky would sit for a few minutes and allow me to admire him as I made baby talk sounds at him. "Good Nicky. What a pretty kitty. Big, big boy, yes you are." That kind of thing. Once I was sufficiently under his spell, he would dash up the stairs and proceed to examine (i.e. walk into, sniff, rub) every room, every corner, even attempting to open (successfully) drawers and secret doors that led out to attic eaves. He would make, essentially, a personalized tour of the entire house. I would eventually run upstairs and fetch him, hauling his enormous warm weight over my shoulder, and carry him to the front door. I waited for that one moment to pick up his soft orange bulk. He never resisted, scratched, or fussed to be let down. I like to think that he actually surrendered for a few moments to my embrace. And then I would gently drop him down onto the front stoop. He would bound off into the day and the rest of the neighborhood, a jungle replete with potential seductions.

The sweet memory of his weight still haunts my arms.

(7)

Tasting the World

Delicious, intimate, and primal—eating and drinking are tasty ways of sampling the world around us. Beyond their survival value—a very big part of the action, I grant you—these acts can be deeply nourishing on other levels as well. Think how much fun it is to feel the crunch of a crisp cracker, or the pleasure of sipping ice-cold lemonade on a hot, muggy day. Flavor is a direct link to our animal origins, but can also lead to some of the most sophisticated and memorable sensations in our lives.

We all have our favorite flavors, like hot tea on a cold, rainy day. The tea brings a steaming island of warmth, gently scented and fragrant with aid and comfort. For so little effort and money, tea can happen anywhere that water can be boiled. Hot tea at the end of a day spent slogging through the rain? There is no greater joy. Ice cream is one of my passions. Think of it: cream frozen and whipped into a gift for the mouth and taste buds. The cold is bracing, exciting, especially since I know if I eat it too fast—which I almost always do—it will lead to an ice-cream headache. But the headache will pass quickly, so I let myself not simply lick, but bite into the scoop of ice cream.

Travel is one of the quickest ways to dive into realms of new foods and flavors. As an adult I looked forward to regional foods and culinary styles as shortcuts to understanding something about the people, their tastes, the things that mattered to them. Italy became a place for spring salads, autumn fresh porcini, gelato consumed daily by *tutti*—every single person capable of holding a cone.

One August afternoon in Milan, I was wandering through the art deco corridors of the Galleria Vittorio Emanuele, admiring the marble inlays in the cafe-strewn sidewalks, when I spied a conveniently located gelateria. My eyes savored the colors of pistachio, lemon, and mint, but my mouth zeroed in on the brilliant pink of amarena—the slightly sour cherries that grow in Italy. Yes, I would like two scoops of that! Somehow the brilliant pink scoop of gelato echoed the architecture of the northern Italian city. It tasted Italian, and so does the memory of that afternoon that returns every time I encounter sweet-tart amarena gelato. Italian foods are about enjoyment of the moment—robust, supple, happy flavors without trickiness and frills. For that, there is French cuisine!

Cold beer for me is forever fused with the indolent pleasures of Mexican beaches. Exhausted from swimming and body surfing, I say yes every time to a cold Corona with lime. How can you beat the perfect match of the bitter ice coldness of the beer and righteous physical weariness on a hot day? These sensations entwine as indelibly as temple ruins, scarlet embroidery, and fresh-caught fish grilled on the beach. Or my mother's brown sugar brownies: one taste and I'm back in her kitchen scooping the warm cookies onto the silvery wire racks to cool.

Hot dogs and bagels came to me via Manhattan. Whipped cream and chocolate, in Holland. Schnitzel and warm potato salad delighted my youthful palate in Bavaria. And I can never forget the earthy fragrance of a pot of roast chicken immersed in rice and chicken juices, served directly from the oven by a red-faced Parisian housewife in spiky high heels. The juicy chicken, the rice soaking up all of its rich, simple flavors accented by aromatics—onion, carrots, celery, thyme.

Let's not forget the negative flavors. Not many, but some. I occasionally revisit liver just to see if I have outgrown the queasy-making ickiness I associate with its pinkish-brown sheen, the slippery tumescence and overripe flavor. So far it hasn't worked. Still, given my many years as a food writer, I have never said no to the offer of something new and unusual Alarmingly large snails on Crete? Uh, yes. I found that with enough garlic they were just fine. Elk. Tough. Wild boar. Gamey but delicious. I've agreed to alligator (but only once), rattlesnake (surprisingly tasty), crickets (with lots of hot sauce), bear (tough), kangaroo (uninteresting), horse (it was on the menu in Genoa; how could I refuse?), quail egg (fabulously rich), raw beets (flavorless), barracuda (oily), goat milk ice cream (farmyard-esque), raw cookie dough (well, you know how addictive that is), and apple cider custard (terrible).

What's better than a new flavor? An old one. Anticipating a favorite dish at a favorite restaurant is one of my absolute pleasures. Jack and I go out to certain places purely in quest of that special thing they do so well. The snapper tacos at El Palomar or the pasta primavera at Tramonti. Flavors can tuck us back into our soft emotional beds, perhaps when we are in need of some extra comfort. My mother used to make tapioca pudding when I was sick and I still associate it with her and her Olympic-grade nurturing skills.

Flavor is an endless highway to social bonding, cultural insights, and the strengthening of deep emotions. That glass of wine with an old friend becomes the richness of the friendship itself. It is the invitation accepted by both parties. The sip exchanged. In the Catholic mass, the symbolic transformation of wine and bread is shared among every person in the room. Oral mysteries are among the very first, the strongest, and most lasting ways we encounter the world.

8

Flavor Collisions

I recently discovered something outrageous: caramel laced with sea salt. The first impression as the teeth sink into this golden-hued (caramel-colored, actually) sticky candy is of chewiness. The teeth plunge into something that offers a playful pushback, teasing resistance. The chewiness could be seen as an obstacle, an unwanted aspect of the candy, but it isn't. On the contrary, the extreme chewiness is part of the joy of caramels. It's a bit of a workout for the mouth and jaws, but then a second stage of pleasure emerges. As I crunch into one of the salt crystals, its saltiness floods into the caramel sweetness, forming a new realm of flavor tension. Finally there's the lingering finish: sweet but not cloying, thanks to the sea salt.

Nothing puckers my mouth in an addictive way like a dill pickle. So irrational is my craving for mouth-puckering sourness that I actually add pickles to other foods and as an accompaniment to even more foods, especially fatty, salty, meaty foods. Ham, for instance, loves to have its rich voluptuous favor cut with the squeaky crisp sour flavor of a pickle.

Hot peppers are an even stranger oral obsession. To consume them is to be made uncomfortable. The hotter they are, the more they question the mouth, and sanity itself. While I never craved hot peppers just for themselves, I've spent many a Thai dinner, napkin at my brow, happily savoring the hyper tingling sensation on my lips and tongue created by the fiery chilies in this otherwise rational cuisine. There's just no accounting for why humans crave these painful condiments: hot sauce, wasabi, horseradish, Serrano chilies, even slightly spicy greens, such as arugula and cress.

Texture can be a tasty mystery, too. Consider the chewy crust, the kind so obdurate, so tooth-endangeringly hard that the loaf in question could be used as a weapon. Yet knowing that there will be warm, rounded, soothing dough flavors inside that tenacious exterior keeps me interested. The contrast is definitely part of the charm.

I adore salt, a fact I learned about myself as soon as my sister and I "improved" the flavor of sour green apples by salting them before eating. I found out about the salty addictiveness of pretzels very early and I have been true to them ever since. I love lemons so much that I do all sorts of things to them to make them friendlier to the mouth. I sweeten lemons into submission or focus on their sour glory, squeezing them into drinks or onto rich foods such as lobster or roast chicken.

Working my way through extreme flavors and textures is a shortcut to knowing something spectacular about the world: I can taste it. Not simply chewy crust, sweet dessert, raw seafood, sour apples, and frozen daiquiris, but there are flavor worlds beyond recognizable, domesticated foods. Think about licking rocks, eating snow, chewing wild sorrel.

The mouth loves contradictions, at least mine does. Flavor collisions and textural non sequiturs make my tongue happy. The tension is the key. Much like a metaphor that holds two competing ideas together at the same time, these sorts of flavor collisions excite an oscillation that can't be resolved. After years of dining out and writing about food, I've discovered that getting to some wonderful flavor can be both arduous and luscious at the same time, for instance, opening up a pomegranate and painstakingly removing the tiny seeds, each one exploding with liquid piquancy. Shelling pistachios, such a hassle, and yet consider the nutty, earthy reward. Many of the best things about exploring the world with our bodies involve tension, opposition, contradiction. Sweet and sour soup. Salted chocolate. It tests my body's ability to fuse opposites, gives my taste buds a challenge to push up against.

When I find a compelling food challenge—the soft cushiony texture of raw tuna wrapped in hot wasabi horseradish—the experience so resonates with my taste buds that they make a perfect fit. Time and again, I've found myself realizing that *here* is a flavor I've been waiting for all my life. My memory has encoded a few priceless flavor encounters and fused them eternally with certain places, people, weather, and celebrations. The discovery of that archaic bitters, Fernet Branca, taught my mouth to forever sing in the key of fermented orange peel. The metallic bite of cilantro on grilled anything makes me smile. And surely salted chocolate was served in the Garden of Eden? To taste a new flavor is to have your body realigned and reshaped. A bit more of the world now dwells inside you.

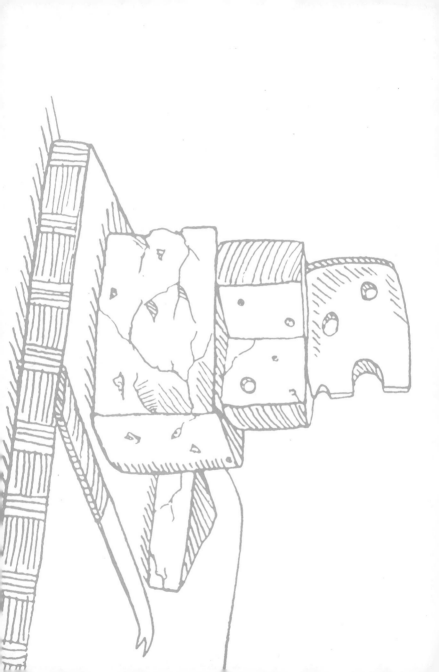

My first taste of Camembert cheese was a voluptuous awakening. That creamy ripe cheese was a flavor I'd been waiting for all my life. Try something you've never eaten before. Have fun with your mouth. Take it for a ride. There's a flavor out there waiting just for you.

your
turn

9

Exploring

"Where are you going?" my mom would ask. "Exploring," I would answer. In the summertime, the entire day was mine to explore. I would rendezvous with two other friends in somebody's back-yard. We'd take a candy bar with us, or an apple—something that helped reinforce the consensual illusion that we were going on an extended and likely arduous trek into terra incognita. After some conversation that often involved raised voices, we would agree on which direction to take that morning. The woods were always a popular arena for exploration. Or across the road—an iffy proposition since our mothers had forbidden us to cross the road. Or along the stream. We'd already been to the stream, but the point of an exploring day was to go farther along that stream, deeper into those woods, or more stealthily across the road in order to gain new information and bring back news of hidden territory, spectacular sights, and perhaps a souvenir or two that would prove without a doubt that we had been exploring.

The most important element of going exploring was that it tempted us out into the larger world, into a place or an experience that was new. My friends and I would become the physical bridge between the known and the unknown, the old and the new, the commonplace and the exciting. We used our bodies to blaze new trails through our expanding world. Later we would use bicycles, and still later, cars and planes to explore the boundaries of our known world, peel back the edges and reveal the fresh, throbbing heart of the new.

Among the obstacles to unfettered exploration were warnings from our parents. Many of these warnings were of the watch-out-for-the-crazy-man-in-the-woods variety, or the stay-out-of-poison-ivy warning, or the perennial don't-stay-out-too-late warning. The warnings added the required spice, the heady whiff of potential mayhem that sweetened each episode of exploring.

59

In Virginia's spacious deciduous woods I encountered new smells, new textures, the gorgeous darkness of forest green. The soft pine needle floors, the sparkling sun held at a distance by the latticework of tall red maple branches and pointed oak leaves. My favorite trail was a wooded path punctuated by ferns and Queen Anne's lace that followed a stream. The path grew vague, ending abruptly from time to time, so I would leave the path and forge ahead through underbrush or over logs, sometimes sliding down steep hillsides. Such freestyle pathbreaking plunged me toward the stream at points. I might find enough big rocks strategically located so I could walk, very carefully, across to the other side. Then I could explore the far edge of the stream, finding—or better yet, creating—a path along its unknown side. Rarely did I return to the same spot to recross the stream. That would mean a retreat back into previously known territory.

When I was younger, living in an old house in Germany, my sister and I could explore within the immediate surrounding of our front yard, a mysterious area bordered by high hedges and a gate in front, and the jungle that was our backyard. What lay beyond that former lawn? What might some close investigation of the yard yield? Some days we would explore with toy shovels or garden spades, like archaeologists looking for fossils and buried treasure. And since the question you ask always determines the answer you receive, sure enough we eventually unearthed a few copper coins, mysteriously encrusted with turquoise oxidation. On one particularly intense afternoon of exploring, our persistence was rewarded by the discovery of two pieces of ancient-looking pottery, little triangles of porcelain bearing decorations that might have dated all the way back to 1935.

In winter, snow covering the paths brought the fresh pleasure of exploring and rediscovery. Where was the path I made last year? Could I find it under all the snow? Trees newly bare turned to pale mauve and silver in the winter light. The stream became a magical expanse of ice, sometimes barely frozen so I could watch the water running quietly beneath the thin glassy veneer. After a week of especially cold temperatures, the stream froze solid, enough to support our bodies attached to ice skates. We could zoom fast over the stream's icy surface, moving farther downstream than we ever ventured in summer. Or we could simply fall down until it wasn't fun anymore and leave off exploring for another day. When summer came around again, torrential rains filled the same stream with a new personality, a raging, muddy, river whose roiling surface rose almost up to the banks. The brave ones among us decided to explore our physical limits by jumping into the muddy froth, floating, scrambling, or riding giant black inner tubes far past the point of permissible venturing. I was often one of them, though my mother was not amused.

Travel is the adult equivalent of going exploring. Even trips to known destinations can bring exploration because all of the everyday routines you count on become unglued and change. I especially love to travel to a new place where I can count on experiencing the unknown, expanding what I know, see, feel, and taste. Exploring requires only that you give yourself permission to encounter something you don't yet know or understand, and that you desire it with the expectation that you will come back changed, perhaps renewed, or at least surprised. Exploring brings us to a place beyond what we can expect and into the midst of something surprising.

your
turn

Drive somewhere you've never been. Visit a new country or state. Walk around a new neighborhood. Find a new place—a building, park, hiking trail, museum, island—and become an adventure tourist. Don't just wave from the car. Get out and get engaged.

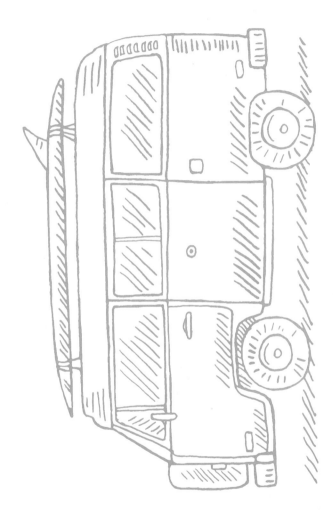

10

The Magenta Jacket

After the dress code shambles of my college days, I settled into a lulling rhythm of professional attire. Sweatshirts and torn black jeans gave way to gray skirts and tights, dressy slacks, and a few substantial sweaters. It all seemed to be working until the day my mother happened to glance into my closet.

"Everything here is black and khaki," she noticed, loudly.

And she was right. It made a kind of practical sense: black is sophisticated and khaki never gives offense. They're the sort of neutrals that fashion magazines always praise, aren't they? Colors that go with everything and never cause any ripples of gossip or behind-the-back laughter. Besides, I liked black and I looked good in khaki, a color which rhymed with my dark blonde hair.

I didn't think about my mother's comment until a few years later when she decided to take me shopping.

"The sales are terrific," she assured me, as we waded into the visual overload of a large department store.

"Here's a great little item!" My mom was holding a chartreuse blouse up to my neck. We looked in the mirror together. The color of the blouse matched my eyes, making them look even greener. Suddenly I appreciated the power of color to flatter key features. But my mother had already flung the blouse back where she found it and was moving briskly toward a sale rack. By the time I caught up with her she had something else clutched triumphantly in her hands.

A magenta linen jacket.

What was she thinking? I wondered. I have never worn magenta, though I loved the way it looked on other people— such a luscious, bold shade of pink.

"Try it on," she urged.

So I did. We both surveyed me in the magenta jacket reflected in the floor-length mirror. "It fits you perfectly." It did. "And it's fully lined." It was. "The price is incredible." Yes, indeed. The $250 jacket had been marked down to $79.95. Was this not a steal for a fully lined linen jacket that fit as if it had been made for me? The gleam in my mother's eyes sealed my fate. My heart sank, but my hand reached for a credit card. I was going to take the magenta linen jacket home.

Many factors swirl around the thorny issue of buying clothes, but common sense is not always one of them. It was true that I had never owned anything in this color. Could I simply be lacking in fashion imagination? In color bravery? Had I been stuck in a clothing rut? Well, no more! The absence of a magenta garment in my wardrobe had been corrected. My horizons had been expanded.

As the years passed, I added more green to my clothing choices. Rummaging around for a winter coat or flannel shirt at the back of my closet, I would occasionally catch a glimpse of magenta. A pang of guilt would strike and quickly subside. I *would* get around to wearing that incredible bargain purchase, surely this coming spring. Or the next one.

You already know what I'm going to say. I never wore the magenta linen jacket. How could I? Every time I tried it on, I winced. The color screamed at me; it mocked me. There was no way I could wear that color out in public. Someone else could, but not me.

I ignored its presence in my closet for a decade until the truth spread over me like a big fat grin. This was a resounding lesson in being clear about what made me happy, what gave me a feeling of confidence; in knowing what was right for me—what fit. The magenta linen jacket joined the royal blue sweatshirt decorated with gold embossed reindeer I'd been given at a gift exchange party, and the faded maroon cutoffs that almost fit, but not quite. They were all hot items at the garage sale my neighbor and I held a few months later.

your turn

Retrieve a neglected piece of clothing you haven't worn in years. Try it on. Give it a moment. Better yet, put it on and leave the house. Be mindful of how you feel wearing it. If, on this outing, you cling to the shadows or dread running into anyone you know, feel free to discard the item. But if you feel a new sense of bravado, keep it. And wear it again.

Washing Socks
in the Mojave

In the desert, Jack and I like to get up while it's still dark, pre-dawn, and get to the trailhead of our favorite canyon walk before the heat begins. The trailhead is easy to get to and while steep, the ascent rewards us with a dizzying roost from which to watch the sun come up and spill across the flat desert floor below. We ascend in indigo shadows and scramble back down in the orange light of morning. Along the way we've seen coyotes, chipmunks, even big horn sheep, and we've admired forests of barrel cactus showing off their coronas of spring flowers. Birds dart in and out of the massive stones. The sound of sun-baked gravel crunching under our feet lives permanently in our bodies. We'd enjoyed many such sunrise hikes on our desert trips, enough to require many pairs of socks.

"So why didn't you pack a few more pairs?" I wondered aloud in fairly pithy tones. But he hadn't, and once I stopped fuming, I felt sorry for him. Feet hate to be stuck inside dirty socks, especially in the heat of the Mojave. So I gathered up two pairs of Jack's dirty socks and decided to submit to what had to be done.

Adding some liquid soap to the funky porcelain sink in our adobe cottage, I filled it with water, submerged the socks, and began swirling them around in the bowl. I could hear the rustling of palm fronds just outside the little bathroom window, the soft scraping and dry metallic whispering of the dried fronds. The tiny bathroom was decorated with its original 1920s tile work and an old-fashioned mirror with a medicine cabinet we never opened. The floor was inset with large terra-cotta tiles that always seemed to attract bits of gravel and sand from our morning and evening treks. I heard the harsh squawk of ravens swooping through the palm trees and telephone poles, bickering over territory. I plunged my hands up and down, in and out of the water, swirling, squeezing, tamping the socks down when they insisted on trying to break the surface and escape. Longing to be out in the dazzling afternoon sun, I was standing in front of a tiny sink surrounded by peeling paint washing socks.

Yet I slowly realized I was enjoying the simple action of washing the socks. My hands were entranced by the rhythm of movements, plunging in and out of the water. The wet fabric in my hands felt entirely different than the feel of dry socks. They became heavier, less like knitted fabric and more like some new entity. I pulled out the socks and let the cloudy water swirl down the drain. Now it was time to squeeze out as much soapy water as possible from the wet socks. They seemed to have expanded and become more like living spongy creatures. I squeezed them extra hard just to let them know who was boss. I replaced the little rubber plug in the drain and added clear water.

Now came the pleasure of rinsing. I put the truculent socks back into the rinse water and swirled them around again. They behaved and began yielding up the last of their soapiness. I took them out again, squeezed out more soap, pulled out the plug, and did a final rinse. Then I took the clean, wet socks outside into the small courtyard so they could dry in the hot desert air. Draping them over the back of a deck chair, I went inside where it was cool to read for half an hour. When I came back out to check, the socks were not only clean, they were completely dry.

Restoring the socks to their clean, fresh state was an act of renewal, a ritual of reviving. Washing clothes by hand put me in an intimate closeness to the wearer of the socks—my beloved. I had taken time and effort to restore the clothing he would wear. Our endorphins are open full throttle when we do physical work. It feels good; the body craves more. Even a single act of physical work done by hand had triggered my body's memory of heightened well-being. The humble and direct activity of washing socks reminded me that I was made to feel my way through the world by hand.

72

your
turn

Give your hands some playtime. Next time you assemble a salad or bake cookies, try dispensing with utensils. Make these dishes entirely with your hands. Mix with your hands and toss with your hands. Notice how the ingredients feel to your fingers, thumbs, and palms.

Transformative Housework

Here's a true confession: folding clothes still warm from the sun or from the dryer is an act that never fails to feel good. It is unabashedly sensuous, hands running along the front of my body, smoothing the folds of the warm fabric, pressing it against my thighs, stomach, and breasts as I even the hems and straighten the seams before allowing half the fabric to fall forward in an exact twin of the bottom half.

I use my teeth to hold the top of a large article of clothing, the way my mother used to do it. With jeans, I hold the waistband with my teeth while smoothing the entire length of the legs down, adjusting the seams so that they meet and then opening my mouth to release the top half of the garment, flip it in half, smoothing and straightening it all the while. When it is folded exactly the way I like it, I release the soft, warm item and place it on top of the growing stack of clothes.

Large stuff is always more fun to fold than small items. Socks offer only the modest reward of being matched and bundled into little balls rather than running rogue one by one. But towels, sheets, and sweaters are treats for the hands and the entire body. If you're not running your hands up and down the warm fabric, and up and down your own body, smoothing, patting, feeling it all as you go, you're just not doing it right. Or more to the point—you're not getting as much as possible out of this ritual magic that is within reach any time you confront a loose, rumpled, unstructured tangle of clothes fresh from the dryer. It is crucial that the clothes still be warm, otherwise they will refuse to become soft and unrumpled. Once cooled to air temperature, they resist your manipulative caresses. Fair warning.

Folding clothes is a meditation of the hands that gives immediate shape and order to your domestic world. Almost nothing is as apt a metaphor for organizing my immediate world, the only one I can actually control. Very few of the global situations and catastrophes I read and hear about daily are within my control. Making sure towels are folded *is* under my control. The neatly folded towels reassure me of the ability of the world to get its act together, using only my hands as instruments of that organization.

Ironing Meditation

I lived in Chip's house for a year while he was on sabbatical in Japan. Chip was a short, slender guy, sleek and fastidious. He loved to wear black and gray clothing, Italian jackets, and French designer glasses. He had a quick grin and meticulous personal habits. Chip's house, a small Craftsman cottage, was exactly like the man. The kitchen gleamed with vintage appliances: shiny Waring blenders, GE toasters, and Hamilton Beach milkshake makers lined up over the antique Wedgewood stove. The walk-in pantry was stocked with jars of homemade jams, chutneys, pickles, and preserves. Everything had a place, every container, can, bottle, and jar was dusted and shiny clean. Most intriguingly, Chip's kitchen one of those fold-down, built-in ironing boards I remembered from my grandmother's pantry.

One day I experimented with the ironing board. It folded down to the exact right height—after all, it was Chip-sized, and so was I. It had been padded and covered with soft cotton. Firing up my iron, I chose something particularly detailed, a blouse with a collar and cuffs and buttons down the front. And I began to iron.

Ironing requires hand-eye coordination, or at least collaboration. As I moved the iron back and forth, I found my hands going to work all by themselves. I felt my eye approving of what my hands had done by means of the hot iron. My hands felt along the surface of the fabric, working as the advance party for the eyes' approval. As I moved the iron over the surface, strategically turning and positioning the garment, an intimacy evolved among me and the blouse and the iron. The blouse progressed from a shapeless, wrinkled mess into a smooth and recognizable garment.

As my hands and eyes performed this soothing meditation, the rest of my body was released from active involvement. My consciousness began to wander. I was able to sense the room curled up around me, to gaze out at the trees, and to observe the progress of the Romano beans and tomatoes in Chip's garden. I admired the voluptuous wall of delicate pink and pale apricot hues offered by the rose bush in front. I was completely without any particular needs, desires, or worries. The time and place were complete, and so was I.

The simple act of ironing had released me into this temporary oasis. Like a bubble suspended in a blown glass globe, I was suspended in a transparent moment in which there was equal pressure on all sides, my hands performing a ritual without beginning or end.

Dusting Meditation

I am convinced of this: dusting is an act of care, and if done with some rearrangement of intention, it can also be an act of renewal. Sure, it can also be an act of drudgery. Dusting is a drag if it has to be done immediately and fast, and dusting the surfaces before a visit from my mother is an act of desperation and anxiety. *Have I missed anything? Did I get all the corners?* But under less stressful conditions, dusting a cherished piece of furniture or the surface of a wooden floor can reveal the beauty of the piece, the very sheen that gives special life to the part of your world it adorns. If the time can be stretched out a bit, dusting is almost like an act of exploration, revealing the long-lost luster, the brighter color, sleeker surface of the shelf, chair, or chest of drawers.

Every time I dust my old English sideboard—a handsome nineteenth-century piece of oak with small drawers and two large interior compartments—running a soft cloth over its curved woodwork, my hands become reacquainted with its rounded bevels and elegant corners. *Greetings, old friend.* I am renewing my regard for this long-standing inhabitant of my home. *See how I love you? How beautiful you are.* It responds by gleaming, revealing the details of its wood, the rich grain and beautiful natural color. It has earned my affection and my personal attention. While dusting, my hands caress this treasured piece of furniture, explore its particular beauty, its age and solid form—dusting this piece is a pleasure for the hand, a small occasion of meditation and remembrance.

(13)

Making Faces

Inga Larsen had it all: legs, looks, and a sexy Scandinavian accent. All the boys mooned over her. All the girls wanted to be her. But I figured out her secret early on: eye shadow. And not just any eye shadow, green eye shadow. A women's magazine I read during my high school days of body image insecurity said that using green eye shadow made blue eyes look even bluer. So *that* was Inga's secret—in addition to being a tall, mysterious blonde. Figuring that the reverse would also work, I ran out and invested in drugstore blue eye shadow to apply on my own green eyes. Thus began a few years of experimentation.

My studies of the grown-up world had made it clear that adult women wore makeup to proclaim their freedom from girlishness. If so, I figured applying makeup to my adolescent face would transform me into a more mature and sophisticated woman. Even though my mother forbade my wearing makeup until I was sixteen years old, I nonetheless sneaked tubes of lipstick, mascara, and eye shadow out of the house each morning and carefully applied them en route to school. Thus transformed I entered the classroom, a magnet (I believed) for female envy and male desire. That I might also be the cause of my teacher's raised eyebrows never crossed my mind. One day an older girl asked me what color eye shadow I was wearing. Success! And even though not a single boy or man has ever complimented me on my makeup, I persist to this day in believing my field-tested theory that makeup makes the woman.

I'm long past the illusion that makeup can compensate for perceived physical flaws. A thick nose might be camouflaged into thinness by artfully applied makeup, but only a camera is fooled. Close up, anyone with eyes notices the makeup trick instantly. Makeup takes time to apply—time, patience, and some skill. If I'm in a hurry, I completely dispense with every artificial additive, except mascara. My eyes look wimpy without lashes coated in black mascara. With it, I am a formidable presence in the world. My eyes are coaxed and heightened into their full, green glory. Take that! my mascara'd eyes say to the world. *I'm ready for you.*

Inga was obviously going for dramatic effect with that green eye shadow. "Look at me!" she was insisting. For me, makeup is a subtler ally, a tool of enhancement. My body is my entry point into the world, which is why I maintain a few rituals of care and maintenance through makeup. My hands move over the surface of my face, as if to reassure each feature of my continuing devotion. A quick glance at the back of the head in the mirror—yes, my hair is reasonably well organized. A hint of blush on the tops of the cheeks brings them into their best focus. I read in that same long-ago women's magazine that it was a good idea to apply makeup the same way every time—first eyeliner, then mascara, then a dab of coverup under the eyes, and finally blusher. And like some advice in magazines, this one has worked for me.

My hands long ago learned this routine, and, as a result, they begin the process all by themselves. My face loves the few moments of attention performed by my hands as I fuss a bit with hair, adjustments of skin tone—those red marks on my nose just won't do! My hands know when I get too carried away with the eyeliner or when the lipstick is too dark to be flattering. The

81

hands are highly aware and conscious. So I let them work and edit the results. The completed effect is one of shiny, fresh reinvigoration. I am ready.

And even if the light application of makeup I allow myself doesn't make a huge visual difference, it is a ritual uniting my personal experience of my body—my hands, face, and hair—with the public body that goes out and stakes a claim in the everyday world. The whole thing is an act of spiritual devotion. I am decorating myself as a sacred artifact, even though I long ago dispensed with the Inga-inspired eye shadow. But I could always change my mind. Makeup is one transformation that can easily be washed off.

Shape-Shifting:
Baking Bread

The first time I attempted bread, I was in my very early twenties. It was in a mountain cabin heated only by a wood-burning stove that was not at the time burning wood. Part of me knew it was too cold in the house for the dough to rise. The other part of me didn't care. I was going to make bread, dammit. I did everything right. I warmed the bowl into which I put the smooth, rounded globe of dough. I put a dish towel over the bowl, and placed it over the pilot light of my gas stove. And I waited. And waited. Desperate for the miracle to occur, I even warmed up the oven and placed the bowl of reluctant dough into the oven, but to no avail. Three hours later, I still had the original ball of heavy, moist dough, nowhere near risen.

Baking bread is not for amateurs. I consulted the experts—bread-baking books, my baking genius grandmother-in-law—and added their wisdom to the lesson of my previous attempt. The next time, I was ready. On a warm afternoon, I assembled the raw ingredients within the confines of a large bowl. Is there anything as amorphous as bread dough? Flour, water, yeast, perhaps some salt and sugar. Raw, simple substances found in most kitchens outside of Asia. They are so loose, these kitchen elements, so unwilling to have some form of their own that they must be corralled into a bowl in order to stay put. It was time to unleash the other catalyst, my hands. The point of making bread is to let the hands explore their power—that and having something heavenly to eat as an extra added attraction.

The warm room helped the dough to rise. My hands helped to knead it back down, in order to coax texture and sheen into the dough. It's such a primitive dynamic, the yeast and the hands, rising and falling, rising again and punching down, until the mass (still shapeless but no longer loose) has just the right elasticity. I punched the dough down with my fist. Ha! What fun it was to play rough with the dough. Of course, there was some waiting for the dough to rise, but it didn't take as long this time, and eventually it was ready to pop into a bread pan and place into the hot oven. Soon the house was suffused with an ancient aroma. My senses did a little dance and my nostrils opened wide. Nervously, I opened the oven door. Had the dough browned, the top risen, the edges pulled free of the pan? I was elated. The formerly raw and uncooperative dough now rose proudly into a dome worthy of Brunelleschi.

I removed the pan from the oven, waited the required but very long ten minutes, and then popped it out onto a wire rack. It was a beautiful color, with a faintly yeasty perfume. I marveled at the miraculous transformation from shapeless goo to golden brown loaf. When I could stand it no longer, I sliced a piece. You've never seen butter pulled out of a refrigerator faster than at that moment. As you've already guessed, it tasted good enough to worship. I had discovered that baking was not only righteous labor involving my hands and a few humble elements, but that the world could be shaped, and reshaped, with a bit of care, patience, and appetite.

15

Hair Colors

Born with pale hair that rapidly faded into dirty blonde, I spent most of my teenage years longing to free the redhead who lived inside me. I suspected that I was originally intended to have distinctive, unusual hair color—a color that would look the way my feisty personality felt. Nature had simply gotten it wrong. No worries about that; chemistry could fix it. And so with the aid first of henna—what a major hassle!—and then a bottle of Clairol Redwood Flame, I transformed myself from the neck up into a creature of high-wattage auburn locks. I was just trying this out, I assured my mother who was stunned when I presented my color-corrected self for her approval.

For several years, I loved my auburn self. My hair color did indeed attract attention, and I soon learned how to dress in colors that worked best with red hair. The maintenance was messy, but I was willing to endure it until one day my sister came to visit me in San Francisco, where I was living at the time with my second husband. Born with thick, lustrous, and dramatically hued raven locks, my sister had never given a thought to changing her hair color. When she was a baby, people would come up to my mother, looking right past me, and ooh and ahh over my little sister's glorious black hair. Vanity set in pretty quickly and she always made sure she kept her hair long and impeccably coiffed.

On the last day of her San Francisco visit, as we were looking at some old photos, my dark-haired sister held up a shot of the two of us and made a bold pronouncement, "Red hair is too strident on you." Her finger pointed to my head in the photograph. "You're really a blonde."

I let out a gasp. I examined the photograph. She was right. My gaudy mane overwhelmed my pale skin and green eyes. My hair color was, in a word, wrong. And though I'd deceived myself that the color looked natural, it was obviously fake, as nobody as pale as I was going to have bright auburn hair.

"She might just have a point," my husband chimed in, not daring to make eye contact.

After my sister left, I made immediate plans to reinstate my own natural hair color (maybe just a bit lighter). The minute the grotesque red, the red that screamed *wrong* was gone, my eyes and skin brightened, returning to their central role in defining the face I presented to the world. I exhaled. I had been living a colorful lie. A lie that was fun, one I had to get out of my system. Returning to the hair color I'd been born with felt surprisingly liberating and a bit of a relief. Coming home to a physical me that alteration hadn't been able to improve made my body feel like a tuning fork striking a deeply familiar chord.

your turn

Do you have any photographic evidence of a body adornment decision you once made and later regretted? Find these images, or if you don't have any, draw a picture of yourself. Savor the other you.

Enjoy, admire, even laugh if you like. Then put them away.

16

The Red Riding Hood Coat

My sister and I never tired of arguing over who got to wear the prized loden green coat. The coat had a hood lined with red velvet and buttons of antler from a forest stag. Bought in Germany, it was a beautiful wool coat, a Red Riding Hood coat. Once upon a time the coat had a sibling, a smaller version that had been purchased for my younger sister. Once she outgrew the smaller one, the bickering began. We had arrived at our early teens and were both about the same size and height. The remaining Red Riding Hood coat fit us each equally well. I contended that it had been purchased for me; therefore it was mine. My sister pointed out that I'd worn it for two years, and now that she was the right size and had outgrown her original child-sized coat, I should let her wear it.

Something about that coat drove us both mad with the desire to have it, to possess the special fairy-tale power it gave the wearer. Inside its velvet interior, we were enchanted. When damp with snow, it gave off a wintry wool aroma—a woodland scent of mountains and moss. I can smell it now.

Then there's my favorite shirt. Hanging on a hook behind my bathroom door is a men's flannel shirt made by Gant—one of those safe, dependable men's brands—that belonged to my graduate school boyfriend. Originally a rich, crimson plaid crisscrossed with dark green and black lines, the shirt is now soft from an infinity of washings. The neck facing is no longer completely attached. The cuffs have frayed beyond repair. Buttons have been replaced countless times. The red has faded into a nameless, un-red hue. But it has been with me for many years. It has kept me warm, made me feel good as only a red shirt can, especially when my mood is anything but "red shirt." In that shirt I inhabit the world's space on my own terms. It is practically an honorary member of my body, comforting and resolutely vintage.

This flannel shirt is a key to how I see myself: practical, sentimental, and resolute. It is an emblem, a wearable reminder of my deep love for lively adventures and turbulent times, then and now. The shirt keeps those important moments from my past close to me now in my present.

My lipstick-red scarf is another cherished item of clothing. Made of tightly woven cotton, I bought it in Mexico City on a trip I took with my dear friend Mr. B for his fortieth birthday. I always feel more confident wearing that scarf. It's so long and substantial I can wind it around my neck three times, creating a halo of glowing red around my face. When I want to be particularly visible, in any sense, I wear that scarf.

The special green coat my sister and I fought over was a coat of fairy-tale dreams. Wearing it, I stepped into a wider world of stories and magic that I still seek in special attire, like the pair of perfectly fitting black pants in which I am immediately sexy, or the chartreuse hooded sweatshirt that transforms me into a young tomboy every time I put it on. Never fails. And my heavy black motorcycle boots allow me to stomp beyond the predictable female persona. (For that, I have the strappy green heels.) Clothing conspires with my body to enter the world in specific ways. Clothes are an immediate world unto themselves, and they also bring the external world right up next to my body.

Clothes tell me how the world feels, the drape of its skin, the heft of its fabric.

Autumn officially arrives each year when I put on that faded red flannel shirt. The provenance no longer matters. It isn't about my ex-boyfriend; the shirt has taken on a life of its own. It suits me. It feels good against my skin. It is warm and just oversized enough to be as comfortable as a shirt can be. As comfortable as an old shirt.

17

Shaping My Space

After spending the first three years of our life together moving from temporary sabbatical housing to more sabbatical housing, Jack and I finally found a small house of our own. It was only a mile from Jack's studio and two miles from the heart of downtown. The first thing I did after moving into our new house was stake out the upstairs back room with its view of the pond for my study. I craved the chance to shape a space utterly my own.

"Why don't you take the larger room, with the higher ceiling?" Jack suggested. But I was drawn to the room at the back of the house, the room that faced the line of trees high above the pond. The view outside the window was soothing, even stimulating. It was the room with a view.

Making the room my own would take time—no space is exactly ideal right off the bat. My office at the university, when I worked as a grantswriter, had taken years of tinkering and adjusting to become truly customized. I wanted the study to be my creative work chamber—a place to work, unwind, and concentrate in. That required careful planning, as well as a few random decisions and spontaneous accidents.

First off, my study needed workspace and a desk large enough for a computer, phone, and lots of papers. I would need good lighting and at least one comfortable chair. Virginia Woolf had a comfortable chair in the room of her own, and so would I. I need to be able to sit at a table, counter, or desk suitable for writing as well as for reading. I like to have a book squarely in front of me, resting on a firm, flat surface, so that I can lean into it as I read. A cup of coffee must be able to sit on the table at my right hand, and there must be room for pens and paper for making notes.

Once the primary requirements for reading and writing were out of the way, I turned to lighting. Should I use an old lamp (continuity), or something new and modern (innovation)? Did I want a tabletop lamp with a moveable arm—which would take up valuable work surface—or a floor lamp with strong, but indirect light that could be moved around the room?

I bought and assembled three wooden bookcases and quickly filled them up (there are never enough bookshelves!) with a combination of beloved classics I wanted to keep nearby and notebooks, favorite music and movies, and photographs. The top of each bookcase cried out for memorabilia. I pinned a nosegay of dried lavender to the wall, under a wood carving of a mermaid from an antique store in Santa Monica that Jack had bought for me on our first trip to Southern California. Atop one bookcase I placed a plastic crucifix collaged with seashells next to a Kachina doll gift from a former teacher, a photograph of me with my father, and a pewter cup filled with watercolor brushes, screwdrivers, and pens. On top of another bookcase I placed a sepia-toned photograph of a great-great-grandfather in a bearskin coat.

The walls began to fill up with special objects either beautiful or filled with important memories. The first item I placed on my computer stand was a dried wisteria pod, its bronze-colored velour softness a meditation for my hands. Silver milagros of feet and hearts purchased on trips to Mexico hung next to one of my first miniature oil paintings of the Mojave. A photo of my grandmother as a young girl gazes at me from an antique oval frame. I tacked up a vintage textile made of geometric patterns appliqued in black and orange, a *mola* made by natives of San Blas in Panama. I've had it in every one of my rooms since I was in high school.

Once a worktable was in place where I could draw, paint, and sew, I added a favorite poinsettia plant to my desktop. The long windowsill behind my desk quickly attracted an incense holder, a piece of volcanic rock, assorted chunks of agate, an abalone shell, and a little glass vase containing pussy willows given to me by my aunt several years ago.

I splurged on a sage green couch that converted into a bed, which I placed against one wall, and found a flea-market Art Deco rug of orange and sage green stripes to cover the hardwood floor. The room was ready for me.

I am not precious about the neatness of my workspace, but I find that once a room becomes too cluttered, my mind starts echoing what it sees. Cluttered space equals cluttered mind. Too many pens, too high a stack of unprocessed paperwork, and I find it hard to concentrate. So I go through the accumulated clutter, throwing things out and trying to file other things away at least once a week. In theory. In reality I sort through the clutter only when it all starts to become a distraction.

A space becomes mine once I make something with it, add something to it, work in it. Ink stains begin to appear, thus customizing an otherwise pristine work surface. I bring in flowers. Flowers wither and dry and then become a visual souvenir in the background. But those background items are critical. They remind me of time passing, of the spring when the flowers were a living bouquet. Same for the matchbook from that restaurant in Rome, a souvenir from a romantic dinner with Jack. The sight of it makes me happy. I couldn't bear to just file it away with other touristic trinkets, so now it sits on the windowsill of my study, resting inside the abalone shell, where I can see it every day when I sit down at my desk to work.

$$\left(\begin{array}{c}18\end{array}\right)$$

The Sunset-Colored Wall

My mother had a great eye for tasteful design. She knew a well-appointed house when she saw one. But it didn't take her discreet nudging and commenting to convince me that the rich colors and deep texture of Persian rugs were not only beautiful but flattering to almost every color scheme and piece of furniture you put on or near them. My eyes loved looking at the interlocking chevrons, hypnotic paisleys, and patterned borders saturated with shades of deep red that adorned rugs from Pakistan, Persia, Turkey, and Syria. The older, the better.

So when I finally had a few nickels to rub together—and my girlfriend's import store was going out of business—I bought one of these richly colored carpets that roughly matched my memories of the sumptuous floor coverings I'd so admired as a girl. It cost a lot. But it lived up to words I have thrown around more than once: *You get what you pay for.* Every day I look at that rug and I smile. It gives me unspeakable pleasure and, indeed, it looks good with whatever is near, on, or above it.

That's how everything around me should look, I decided. And that's how my immediate surroundings should make me feel. If an object doesn't add to my sensory well-being, it doesn't belong. Early on I decided that I was one of those who fell squarely into the camp of the classics. I always went for the timeless and classic, usually (ugh) with prices to match. So whatever I bought usually lasted me for years, sometimes many years.

The knack for developing a signature look doesn't always require money. Simply keeping a sharp lookout for the odd but strangely familiar will do. Beautiful weeds, dried and arranged in eye-catching niches have enriched my living space since my college days. Sea lavender, dried to a poetic and nuanced hue, sits in a raku-fired pot in my office. A wreath I made from pink peppercorns—a gift from my mother's pepper tree—is my favorite front door ornament during the holidays. A single enormous ball bearing, picked up on a tour of an abandoned airbase, sits on my bookcase. Visitors admire it, all eyes seem drawn to its unusual beauty.

It's not so hard to surround yourself with colors, shapes, and objects that you love.

I recall my mom making a daring decision many years ago, when she and my father were helping his parents renovate their living room. It was a rambling old post-WWI house with handsome built-in bookcases, a long, low window seat with upholstered cushions, and a welcoming fireplace that was the centerpiece of the high-ceilinged living room. For as long as I could remember, the interior walls and woodwork had been a nice, neutral ivory color. You know, nothing threatening or weird. Safe.

But my mother saw further. She wanted the room to have new life, something that might delight and enliven the hearts and minds of its aging inhabitants. Within two days the walls glowed a rich, vibrant vermilion—the color of salmon sashimi, of coral, of Marilyn Monroe's lips. It was a gorgeous color, but much brighter, daringly brighter than ivory. With a nod to tradition, my mother kept the trim, floorboards, and wainscoting the original tasteful ivory.

When the walls and woodwork were finished, my mother took the Victorian oil painting of a brilliant sunset over the ocean that my great-grandmother had painted and hung it back up over the fireplace. My father, my sister, my grandparents, and I just stood there, silent with admiration. We were spellbound by what my mother had already seen. The clouds trailing above the ocean, reflecting the glow of the setting sun, were the same shade of vermillion as the freshly painted sunset-colored wall. Such a simple change, yet how daring and how absolutely right.

I never forgot that moment. I vowed, in the fervent, semiconscious way of kids, that I too would expand my list of permissible decorating choices to include something wildly improbable. I too would make an ally of color.

your
turn

Ever gone wild with a new color or piece of furniture that represented a radical departure from your predictable style? Why not? Even if you decide ultimately that turquoise is wrong for your bedroom, take a chance anyway. It's only paint. Color has a way of stimulating new feelings, new freedoms. Start small and see where it leads.

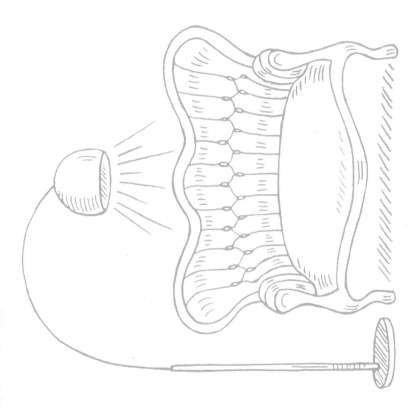

(19) Sleeping Outdoors

After many years of sharing a room with my sister, I was thrilled to finally have my own bedroom. Partly for sleeping, mostly for privacy, my bedroom was an enclosed sanctuary fitted to my specifications. It was my home base, and it provided both comfort and safety. Sometimes, too much safety.

Where we sleep is our choice in some private, primal sense that has no name. Our bedroom is our most familiar space. And so it can be delightful, strange, exhilarating, and frightening—all of those at once—when we allow ourselves to sleep in other spaces. Remember the fun of sleeping over at a friend's house? Part of the thrill was venturing outside the comfort of your own bedroom.

My sister and I used to drag an old mattress out onto the otherwise unused balcony some misguided architect had slapped onto our suburban split-level home. We would bring our pillows, and maybe a snack, with the intention of spending the night. We would then await adventure we were convinced would arrive simply because we were sleeping in a new spot, out under the stars. Those evenings usually ended after only a few hours, after we discovered that we loved sleeping outdoors—just not together. We each became so aware of the other's sleeping sounds, or squirming, that the whole point of being open for neighborhood adventure was undermined.

One night we left the mattress outside after we had retreated to the sanctuary of our separate bedrooms, and the next morning we found its soggy corpse destroyed by an overnight rain shower. Both my sister and I were relieved at the loss of the mattress. We never repeated that particular experiment in sleeping space.

Sleeping outdoors was the most adventurous of all. The first time I slept outdoors in a tent was almost unbearably exciting. No walls to protect me. No doors to keep out unknown shapes and entities. And even though my tent was surrounded by other tents, each one containing pairs of Girl Scouts on a woodland weekend, I easily convinced myself that for an entire night I was sailing through the dark forest with unseen animals, night birds, rustling branches, and possibly even genuine ghosts.

103

I've done a lot of camping, backpacking, and wilderness vacationing since those Girl Scout days in Virginia, and in every case I found that sleeping in a tent was only interesting because it gave me quick access to the huge continuous space of the outdoors. The flap of a tent seemed easier to remove and pass beyond than a doorway leading to a hallway within the confines of a house.

A tent also allowed me to be surrounded by the nighttime nonhuman world. Just outside the tent were the faint rustlings of unknown animals, birds, and insects. The shriek of an owl unzipped the darkness and inserted sudden moments of electricity. The fireflies were the most visually magical. (Their glowing enchantment was one of the things I missed when I moved west.) The hum of crickets rose and fell against the low, rippling hiccup of frogs, a nighttime chorus that helped to blanket my sleep with an exotic otherness. Not normal nighttime.

Even better was sleeping outdoors in the open air. Even with my eyes closed I could feel the pressure of the stars upon my body. And with my eyes open, my body seemed to float suspended within the night itself. It's a feeling of complete buoyancy that no indoor space can ever match.

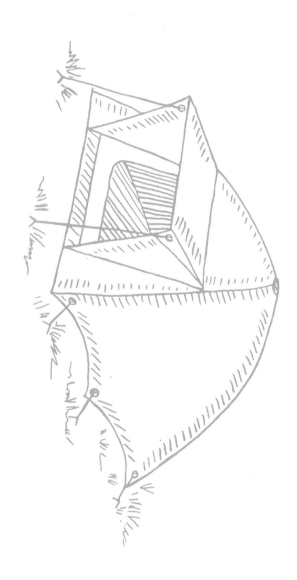

your
turn

Spend a night outdoors, out of your comfort zone. Drag a mattress onto your balcony or deck, or pitch a tent in your backyard. Listen to the night sounds, and try to identify the animals and birds you can hear. Do you remember the name of any constellations? Make some up.

20

Dining by Candlelight

We were crazy in love and didn't really care what we were eating, just as long as we sat across from each other every night and held hands, soaking up the gleam in each other's eyes by candle-light. My sweetie Jack and I both knew that nothing heightens the atmosphere of romance—for lovers, and for the world—like candlelight. Lighting candles took no effort, cost very little, and was a practice which was endlessly renewable.

Candlelight seemed called for during our first dinners together, and we never stopped. If I was cooking, Jack would light the candles. I loved watching his hands holding the flame over the wick, as one by one the candles sprang to life. When he was designing a salad, I lit the candles. Every single meal we've had together at home has been shared by candlelight. Candlelight can overcome a multitude of gaffes. Not enough pasta sauce, spilled wine, stained napkins, burnt baguette, bad hair day—none of that matters if you're surrounded by the glow of candles.

We started off with votive candles, cheap and easy. They also didn't obstruct the view of each other's faces we desired. We soon graduated to tapers, locating odd and endearing can-dlesticks that were among our very first purchases as a couple.

Today fifteen years later, our dinners can require up to a dozen candles, a mix of votives and tall tapers, usually ivory colored, but sometimes in shades of sage green or cinnamon.

Dining by candlelight became a ritual we both loved, one that fit perfectly into our shared life. A flame at the end of a cylinder of wax, candlelight is a living creature animated by the alchemy of fuel and combustion.

When Jack and I light candles at our table, we are in touch with countless acts of sacred commemoration as well as the humble need for light in the darkness. Dining by candlelight connects us with millennia of unknown ancestors who dined by candlelight because they had no alternative. The ritual of lighting the candles is rich with residue of the sacred, the primal, the votive. It's an offering, a vow, a wish, an unvoiced prayer: *May we always dine together.*

I love the way candlelight is just bright enough to create an intimate space for two. It defines that space, turning any old amorphous somewhere into a special here.

Early in our relationship, Jack and I lived in a neighborhood where our dining room window looked out onto a green lawn and beyond that a winding street that connected us with our neighbors. One particular neighbor would ride by on his bike, many evenings each week, on his way home from work. After several months of this routine, we encountered him on the street. Stopping his bike, he asked, incredulously, "Do you really dine by candlelight every single night?" We both grinned and said, "Yes, we do." With raised eyebrows, he rode on. I've often wondered whether he too now dines by candlelight. I like to think so, our candle lighting his, connecting us not just for each other but to the world around us.

your
turn

Light a few votive candles on your table at breakfast.
Does the toast taste any different?

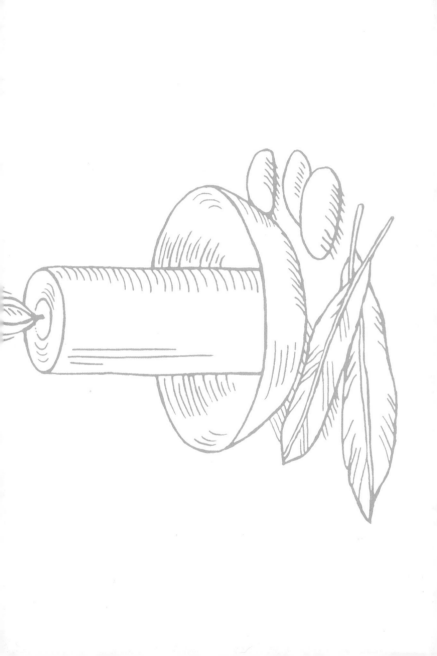

$$\left(21\right)$$

Rites of Memory: Old Sweaters and Cowboy Belts

Childhood treasures, cherished clothes, college notebooks, empty perfume bottles still haunted by the scent of romance—these objects keep us whole. They are our history, kept close at hand, available to open and touch once more. Without our past we have no identity, no continuity. Part of who we are still lingers there.

The earrings my Uncle Bud brought me back from a trip to Tokyo are the old-fashioned screw-on kind, with a circle of green enamel leaves and a filigree of gold petals tipped with amethyst. I don't wear them. I keep them tucked away in a special place with other memory items, and when my eyes see their purple flowers and miniature leaves, I am seeing my younger hands touch Uncle Bud's hands as he gives me the gift. I am with him again, though I am now older than he was when he gave them to me. He has been gone for more than twenty years. I am smiling as I write this; it is such a sweet memory I can feel it in my eyes and my arms. The memory makes me sigh.

The earrings bear a precious freight of both memory and continuity. I am that young girl; she lives within me and she comes out as often as I look at those earrings. Memory is a way in which the world—the world as I was, the world as *it* was—touches us. Memories come to us, tap us on the shoulder, and force us to turn around. Even more often, they permeate the everydayness of our lives and weave in and out so that the texture of any given hour will shimmer and throb with the past (memories), the present (what my hands are doing now), and the future (where I need to be in an hour, what I will be eating for dinner, the trip to Oregon next month).

In my imagination I can see exactly where I put that worn cowboy belt studded with glass gems. I have it safely tucked into the top drawer of a dresser that lives inside my closet. In my mind's eye I open the drawer and see the little drawstring pouch that contains that old childhood treasure, the cowboy belt that used to belong to my cousin Danny and that somehow was given to me. Or did I "borrow" it?

Oh, it's too wonderful a treasure; I stop imagining it and actually walk into the closet, open the drawer, and take out the belt, coiled like a snake of summer dangers and adventures.

The surrealist filmmaker Jean Cocteau tells a story in his diary, *Journal d'un inconnu,* about returning to the house where he grew up in Paris. He filled his eyes with the view of the front door, the deeply framed windows and the long hedge that lined the front walkway. But somehow it didn't touch him; the experience wasn't delivering the deep memory surge he was after. Then he had a brainstorm. He knelt down to roughly the height he would have been as a kid living in that house. He ran his hand along the wrought iron fence in front of the house, and like a needle in an old phonograph record, his body instantly filled with the memories. They came flooding back to him through his child-height hand touching the fence.

I keep that beloved cowboy belt coiled up, since I believe that to be its natural state. The minute my eyes land on the engraved metal buckle I smell the warm redwood dust of the backyard at my uncle's house. Perhaps there's some salty sweat and motor oil mixed in. My hands line up with the grooves of the buckle and run along the scratched curves of the leather to the little glass studs. They are now dulled with time, use, and the sticky grasp of young hands through many games and hours of play. Yet their original hues—royal blue, scarlet, emerald green, and amber—still remain through the scratches. The belt had been stored away during our adult years, until found, and lost, stored and found again through a series of moving days and new homes, until it has been returned to my care, a little worse for the wear. Those summers remain for all time in that little leather belt, formerly my cousin's and now mine. A worn leather reliquary of our youth.

Another rite of memory involves running my hands along the oversized bumps of an intricate knitting pattern constructed decades ago by my mother during one of her knitting frenzies. She would crank out these big nubby cotton pullover sweaters in toffee and caramel colors for my sister and me. We loved their bohemian nubbiness, and we wore them and wore them, and then inevitably moved on to other clothing, other sweaters, other textures. But the sweaters were so eternal and plush with my mother's touch that they had to be kept, stored, never given up.

Even though I never wear them, I still have two of these nubby, texturally extravagant sweaters. I can feel them right now, even though my fingers are actually moving briskly over the spun aluminum keys of my computer keyboard. Yet the sudden visual impression of my mother's hands flying along the yarn is so potent it can weave its way back into my body through memory alone.

When touched, the actual sweater opens even deeper canyons of recollection, nostalgia, and the heft and weight of many tactile pleasures. The rows of knitting unlock that place, that person and all of the feelings, yearnings, laughter, perhaps, a smile—yes, definitely a smile—and the happiness of wearing a handmade garment that made me feel warm, but even more, made me feel loved.

22

Fresh Peach Pie

My dad loved taking us on all-day driving trips, usually on a Sunday, and usually in the direction of some historical landmark. Gettysburg was a favorite destination, especially in late summer. One year he set off for the historic battlefield countryside, and after a day wandering among the hallowed hills, sitting atop cannons and pausing to consider the intricacies of that war, we started home the long way, crossing the Maryland state line near the heart of Amish country. A handwritten sign caught my father's eye and the car seemed to steer itself onto a narrow dirt road.

Fresh pie. That's what the sign told my father, and the boy in him responded. The car rolled up to a small table stand shaded by a canvas awning. Two women wearing white Amish caps, simple black dresses, and aprons stood smiling. They liked the looks of my handsome dad and he liked the looks of the fresh pies laid out like Tiffany jewelry under the awning.

He had already eaten half a slice of the homemade pie by the time he waved us out of the car to come see for ourselves. Upon further questioning from my father, the women revealed that they also had homemade ice cream and root beer. Nearby. We stood happily in the warm day, under the shade, and feasted on fresh peach pie made from the harvest of their orchards and vanilla ice cream made from milk from their cows, while the Amish women watched with smiling faces.

A bushel of peaches came home with us that day, peaches my father could not stop eating until he was practically sick. The remaining peaches my mother, sister, and I peeled, sliced and made into pies to be frozen in the downstairs freezer. A few months later, in mid-October, we took out a pie, baked it, and consumed it with unrestrained pleasure. We recalled the wonderful drive up into the orchards, the heat, the ice cream, the women in their modest black dresses, and the bursting, fragrant juices of those ripe peaches.

Food is a delicious pathway to social joy. Enter a house almost anywhere in the world and you'll be offered something to eat. Eating together is a quick and direct way of making friends, with the earth and with other people. There's a reason celebratory meals, shared with lots of people around a large table, are such universal rituals. Imagine a Seder without the food, a wedding without the cake and champagne. It's just not possible.

At an organic farm dinner just south of San Francisco last summer, I joined dozens of others sitting at long tables set out in the fields between redwood-forested mountains and the sea. I sat near the end of the table, where I could watch the stand of cypress trees turning deep sunset orange. Purple pears ripe enough to pick brushed against my shoulders.

"It was our best pepper harvest in years," the sunburned farmer told me, passing a plate piled high with red and yellow peppers glistening in olive oil and fresh basil. The man in the straw hat next to me, and his wife across the table, had driven up from Los Angeles for this special dinner. They told me they'd always wanted to share a meal out in the growing fields, with the people who grew the produce. Their faces shone.

"We're in the right place," he smiled, passing the plate down to the folks nearest the rows of sunflowers, tall and heavy with seeds. Here we were, sitting inside a Van Gogh painting.

Standing up and striking his fork against his wineglass to get our attention, the farmer looked down the long rows of assembled guests.

"I want to thank you for coming out here and sharing some of our harvest with us," he said. I reached for more roast chicken, and helped myself to braised fennel and artichokes from another aromatic platter. The man in the straw hat moaned with pleasure as he dipped his artichoke leaf into a garlicky sauce.

"The wines came from grapes just up that hill," the farmer continued. "Let's toast the winemaker!"

A tall man with a ponytail, wearing a tweed jacket and blue jeans, stood and beamed, as we all applauded, raising our glasses filled with his handiwork. Sitting down again, the farmer turned to me and whispered, "I don't think I can eat another bite." Now it was my turn to laugh. We all ate another bite, and another, until the slices of Meyer lemon cake and fresh berries arrived—picked from the patch I could see over my left shoulder.

I pulled my shawl around my shoulders, leaned over to give hugs to the man in the straw hat, his wife, and the farmer, and made my way back to my car in the twilight.

Thanksgiving comes with rewards and challenges for every family. One year around my parents' oval table, the large group included my sister and her boyfriend Steve, my acupuncturist friend Laurel, a few neighbors, and my dad's historian buddy, Pete, and his wife. One challenge always involved my dad's insistence on carving the turkey. My mother's turkeys tended to be dry, and we could never quite figure out why.

"Don't worry, Mama," I reassured her. "I made plenty of gravy."

Dry or not, the turkey looked perfect. Once it occupied its place of honor, my dad made a big show of sharpening up the

115

carving knife with the antler handle he'd bought in Switzerland, and proceeded to hack the bird into wildly irregular shapes. My mother always seemed surprised at his lack of carving skills, and she always protested, "Don, don't just throw the turkey on the plates!" But he always did, and he had fun doing it.

My sister and I barely suppressed chuckles. Poor Mama. As the pie course arrived, the subject of Pete's bursitis came up.

"Have you ever considered acupuncture?" Laurel asked. He hadn't.

"I have my needles out in the car," she said. "Would you like me to give you a short session?"

My father gripped his chair. He whispered to me, "What is she going to do?"

By the time I'd finished my pie, Pete's left forearm was covered with a thicket of tiny silver needles.

"Give it some time," Laurel advised Pete, and started on her second piece of pie.

My mother nudged me and looked over at my father. His face was drained of color.

"Laurel, perhaps it would be better to continue your session another time," I said, raising my eyebrows in warning. Later, after the guests had gone and my mother and I were washing dishes, my mother revealed my father's lifelong aversion to needles.

"At least the turkey wasn't dry this year," I said. My sister and her boyfriend giggled uncontrollably in the next room.

My favorite meals are the ones that defy categories. Sometimes even the simplest meal shared by two people can take on mythic, or at least memorable, proportions.

When Jack and I were falling in love, we often drove out of town to an atmospheric (ramshackle) diner perched at the edge of the cliff. From the front porch of The Whaler, we could see the ocean, which always added an extra dollop of atmosphere to our already quickening romance. (A romance in full bloom to this very day.) It was our little hideaway spot. When Jack asked me where I wanted to have dinner on my birthday, I instantly replied, The Whaler.

But by the time we arrived, the kitchen was closing. Was there anything we could order? French fries, they told us. So that's what we had. Jack and I took glasses of red wine and a plate of salty fries across the highway and out to the edge of the cliff. Dangling our legs over the edge, we plied ourselves with wine and fed each other French fries until every single star had settled into the sky.

Making an Impression

I never met a field of snow I didn't want to impress. You know what I mean—a field of snow on which to throw myself down and fling my arms out wide. Moving them back and forth I clear a semicircle shape out of the white snow, making a snow angel with my body.

My body has learned a lot about its limits, as well as all the fantastic things it can do, by pushing against the material world. Testing, feeling, pressing. The surfaces I approached often met me halfway. *Sure you can push on me,* a muddy stream bank responded. *I'll let you reach in below the surface—but only so far.* Other surfaces let me know they were in charge. Rocky cliffs refused to be impressed. Bodies of water allowed me immediate entrance, even though it was on their own liquid terms. How could I learn unless I set out to touch and probe?

As a kid I couldn't resist leaving a trace of my body anywhere an impression could be made. My young hands gravitated toward wet clay (even wet cement). The chance to leave a unique impression of my hands or initials captured for all time was just too tempting.

Sometimes just being in exactly the right terrain creates impressions without even trying, a sandy beach, for example.

My feet love leaving prints in moist sand (or messy oval shapes in warm, dry sand). Footprints in the sand are a small trace of our presence and a reminder of our impermanence. Here today, say the footprints. Gone tomorrow, says the incoming tide.

Even if the imprint is temporary—snow will inevitably melt, concrete can be smoothed over, beaches are washed clean by the tide—the impromptu action is the important thing. Pushing our bodies into the earth, into some sudden malleable substance, we test our own weight, our own existence. See? There's my footprint. Proof of my unique body. When we're young, it's a way of testing just what having a body, being in the world, really means. Obviously I am here, I exist unmistakably in this moment. The footprints tracking my movements like small bas-relief shadows prove it. For a short time, thanks to my foot marking the sand, I can actually watch myself move through space.

119

The allure of these temporary impressions is their ephemeral nature, a metaphor for the transitory nature of all things. I'm still hooked on watching the imprint of my feet walking along the sand, to be gradually erased by the tides. Like listening for an echo until it fades into nothingness, I watch, mesmerized, as the impressions dissolve. Magic every single time.

(24)

Muddy Day

I was three thousand miles from home, living in the San Francisco Bay Area woods with an absentee husband. I had come to his corner of the world after graduating from college. Mistake. I had neither job nor car, while he still had the job he'd had for many years. Big mistake. Instead of admitting to myself how lonely and homesick I was, I plunged into my new role as a stay-at-home wife, determined to stay busy with the brand-new adult business of keeping a house and garden in decent shape.

I tried to plant vegetables, but nothing would grow in the deep shade of the forest encircling our small house, a former vacation cottage deep in the woods. So I tended the ferns that grew without restraint and fed the chickens I raised in the back— they seemed to be able to grow just about anywhere.

The interior of the little house was the next obvious place to exhaust my emotional turmoil. I repainted the kitchen. I hand-stitched embroidery on colorful comforters, learned to sew my own clothes, and baked bread until I gained enough weight to require a larger size of jeans. I made new curtains for every window. Growing more heartsick each day, I played guitar, painted, made ceramic tchotchkes, and refinished an antique dresser. If there was a surface within reach, I had scrubbed, rearranged, resurfaced, and adorned it until I was blue in the face.

In late autumn the rain began and wouldn't stop. The rain pouring down the windowpanes and falling in sheets from the eaves soaked through my denial. I was depressed, bored, and angry. What had I done? Why was I here, without friends, meaningful work, or any of my familiar passions? Feeling sorry for myself and at the end of my fix-up-the-house rope, I went out onto the front porch and confronted the mud. The soaked earth had given up trying to ooze away from the front steps. It just hung around getting thicker and thicker as the hours went by.

And then finally the storm passed. I sat on the front sidewalk, ignoring the wet concrete and my bare feet, and considered my pathetic situation, filled with self-pity and with no one to blame but myself. Throwing aside the rulebook of adult behavior, I responded in the only way possible: I made mud pies.

Grabbing handfuls of the wet, chocolate-colored earth, I began shaping the mud into baseball-sized globs, neatly laying out the results on the sidewalk. I had made about six of them when I realized that the process required more artisanal spin. I grabbed one of the mud balls and began to squeeze, pat, and shape it into more of a mud patty, wide and round in circumference, but smooth and pressed flat. My hands were so happy grabbing the oozing mud. Forming, feeling, and shaping the mud was wildly liberating, and all the more fun because there was no sensible end result in sight. Gone was the tight hard feeling in my heart. My emotional peace had returned through a playful bodily experience; my hands had opened an unexpected back door that allowed my feelings of isolation to escape.

I was able to make a few key decisions after the day of the mud pies. I soon moved away from those rainy woods feeling lighter and open to the world. I recall those days as a tough yet crucial passage to a future I could live with, and live in.

My hands still squirm with pleasure at the sight of mud.

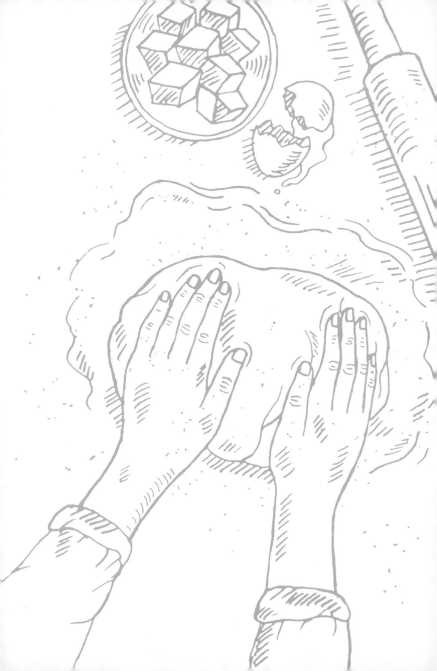

Do something spectacularly messy, on purpose. Mix
up a batch of cookies using your hands. Eat with your
fingers. Buy a set of finger paints. Next time it rains, go
out and take a walk—no umbrella or hat—just you and the
downpour from above. Doesn't messiness feel great?

25

Purposeful Wandering

"Let's see where this road goes," my father would often say. Sometimes, I'll admit, it was after my mother had failed as a navigator. My father would then pretend that the car was steering itself toward an unknown destination. Terra incognita. Such excitement. We had turned into adventurers in an otherwise known and humdrum world.

Getting lost was an excuse to feel electrifyingly alive. Every fiber and cell in my body tingled. I was fully activated and on watch, looking around to see what the unknown road and its unknown destinations had to offer. What lay ahead? What would we find?

Sometimes being lost lasted only as long as the next gas station, where we would pull in and ask for directions. My father would get out and have an impromptu conference with some adult who looked like he knew the territory. Then he'd return to the car, brimming with confidence. He and my mother would exchange looks; he would point to a particular spot on the map she was holding. Then he'd turn smoothly out of the parking lot, back onto the road and we would proceed. We weren't lost anymore. We'd found out where we were and where we were going. Now things felt a bit dull and ordinary. But why?

What is the allure of getting lost? I can still feel it in my body, a faintly sickish excitement. Little needles of energy would start throbbing along the shoulders and back, sometimes in the hands, and a flush would spread across my cheeks and forehead. I would feel my pulse increasing, my blood speeding up, a rising tide of anticipation. Being lost—even the remote suggestion of being lost—immediately set up a force field of anticipation. Something unknown, unplanned, or even unpleasant might occur. And where there was an unknown, there were expanded possibilities.

When you know where you're going, you have set up a controlled series of actions. I'm going to London, so I know I have to take a certain plane, and then a cab, and finally walk into a certain hotel on a certain street. All known in advance. It's true that along that known trajectory a lot can happen to inject surprise, unexpected encounters, delightful discoveries, and even a few disasters into the mix. But you probably won't end up in Cincinnati or Moscow.

I'm talking about situations where you start out for London and get on the wrong plane that takes you to an airport in Iceland where you meet some friendly people who offer you overnight lodging and turn out to be filmmakers whose next movie will star you playing a sixteenth-century Viking princess. See what I mean? Getting lost can generate an infinity of possible ways of being "found."

I admit there have been times when that wrong turn led to unpleasant situations, but other times, the accidental shortcut led through a small sleepy village almost forgotten in the rush to take faster, newer roads. Being able to successfully navigate lostness—a bit of a contradiction in terms, I'll grant you—was always a chance for me to feel fearless, to test my skills with direction and instinct. Did it feel right to follow this road a bit longer? Was the sun over my left shoulder when I turned off the known path? Learning to follow the sun, to notice landmarks—the forested regions, which side the ocean is on, the high mountain peak—helps me orient myself. And one of the greatest pleasures of being lost is getting found. Rediscovering where you are is much sweeter if you have to work for it.

I like to indulge in a variation of getting lost that I call "purposeful wandering." That's the mode of experience I enter when I decide to take some unknown path or road and see where it leads. It's a variation on exploring, that staple of my youth where every day led to some tiny corner of an unknown place or activity.

126 Purposeful wandering requires a bit of unscheduled time. You need to be able to lose at least a few hours, and ideally an entire day. Then you don't have to curtail or edit or inhibit your inquiry. Purposeful wandering requires trusting your own skills and smarts. No one wants to wander off the beaten track unless they think they can negotiate a few bumps on the road or talk their way out of a rough patch. Wandering takes some confidence and a big handful of interest in what lies ahead. The path not taken, yes, but also the willingness to engage in freestyle living, not knowing exactly what will come next.

And what is the payoff for this sort of chutzpah? New awareness and a new feeling about yourself. You learn how far you can go, and you find out things you never would have any other way. The hidden grove of eucalyptus trees blanketed in Monarch butterflies. The old barn with one crumbling wall, just around the bend from an estuary filled with white egrets. Woods filled with oak and elm trees, wild irises, and streams swollen from recent rainstorms. Your feet weary and sore because they took you so far in a single afternoon.

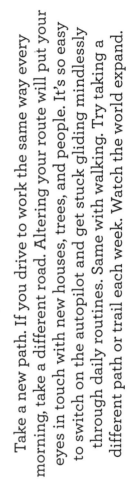

your
turn

Take a new path. If you drive to work the same way every morning, take a different road. Altering your route will put your eyes in touch with new houses, trees, and people. It's so easy to switch on the autopilot and get stuck gliding mindlessly through daily routines. Same with walking. Try taking a different path or trail each week. Watch the world expand.

Hero Mom

My mom never said no if I wanted her to sew me a new skirt. I could always bring a friend home for dinner during the summer; my mom always found a way to stretch the salad or locate another piece of chicken to throw onto the BBQ she managed so well. She would drive me to music lessons or swimming practice. To this day, former boyfriends of mine recall her legendary tuna fish sandwiches, with oversized origami layers of lettuce and micro-diced celery for extra crunch in every bite.

My mother was combination tailor, chauffeur, cook, and maid, always unexcitingly there, just off center stage, which was reserved for my father, my sister, and me. She didn't have a day job, so my sister and I assumed she was there just for us. For most of my young life, before I left home and went to college, I thought my mom was typical of all moms. I thought everybody's mom was part of the comforting, resourceful, but not-too-dramatic furniture of growing up. It wasn't until I was an adult that I realized many of my friends had grown up in very different situations.

My dashing, handsome father was the center of excitement in our family. A tennis pro and sportsman, he'd flown dangerous, rickety, single-engine planes as a teenager and was always at the ready when a strong pair of hands was needed. A professional engineer, he oozed expertise, and I idolized him.

If I had to pick a moment when I was thrust out of my unthinking view of my mother as sweet, pliable wallpaper, it was one autumn day when I was roller-skating with half a dozen of the neighborhood kids. We were hanging around the little cul-de-sac at the end of our street, practicing figure eights on our roller skates, when we heard a shriek. Ken, a skinny little kid whose older sister Dianne was one of my buddies, had been skating too fast for his beginner-level skills and had crashed into the jagged edge of the curb. There was lots of blood and tears and whimpering. My mom came running out of the house and made the grim assessment: Ken had broken his arm. Then came something my eyes could barely believe. My mom grabbed the morning paper, which was still sitting at the edge of the driveway, and turned it into a makeshift splint.

My mom told us Ken needed to get to a hospital to have his arm looked at. But the only vehicle among our immediate neighbors was a manual transmission, somebody's second car whose owner was at work. A few other mothers were at home, but not one of them could drive stick shift—except my mom. I never knew she could. Without missing a beat, she and another adult picked up Ken, put him in the backseat and away my mom went, driving a borrowed car that required expertise with a clutch and four-on-the-floor gearshift.

The moment etched itself in my young consciousness. My homemaker mother had saved the day. She never hesitated. A situation was put in front of her and she dealt with it. Somehow, somewhere, she had acquired the skills that would equip her to handle an alarming accident with confidence. She had the firm, clear abilities that made life easier, that got broken-armed little boys to the hospital.

That incident forced me to revise my narrow assessment of my mother. I came to expect more from her, expecting her to be

131

strong, tough, and capable in the world beyond her well-tended domestic turf. I'm still amazed when my mom sheds her predictable, comforting identity. She doesn't do it too often—only when it matters.

I made a note to myself that day: *Be that woman.* My mother taught me, if life offers you the skills to reach further, to spring into action when others might need you—swimming, making a fire in the rain, giving CPR, installing a smoke detector, driving stick shift—jump in and learn.

PART TWO

how the world
touches us

27

In Bed at Dawn

One morning I awoke to a chorus of frogs. Their machine shop vibrations broke through my sleep and forced me awake. I didn't move; I listened. Weaving through the vocal energy of the frogs came a glissando of birdsong. The red-winged blackbirds that populate the reeds around the nearby pond were waking up and filling the morning sky with a filigree of melodic waterfalls.

The night before I had decided I would not rush out of bed in the morning. I would not race to the gym for my daily contest with an elliptical strider. I would stay in bed a few indulgent minutes longer. And in those minutes it dawned on me how perfectly my body had adjusted to the bed, how the bed was shaped around me. It was a priceless moment, with equal pressure on all sides: body, bed, temperature, and the precise organization of the pillows and sheets—soft cotton sheets that had long ago been washed smooth to the point of weightlessness. Since my feet need to feel snug at night, I always let them enjoy the light pressure of my patchwork quilt. The reassuring weight of that quilt seemed to float above my body by dawn.

Our tight embrace with planet earth is most immediately felt in the body's lifelong alliance with gravity. The sense of sinking in, of relief, of abandoning oneself to exhaustion and end-of-day quietude happens when we exchange standing on our feet for lying down in our own bed.

No matter how high we jump, we can only jump so high. Gravity pulls us back. We belong to the earth—that's the basic message. Perhaps that's why lying down, especially full-bodied stretched out, feels like a glide back into infancy, to our first moments of being in touch with the world. In lying down we feel the support of the world. Our earth supports us when we walk, run, and sit. Yet these acts require us to make an effort to maintain certain postures; we need to fight, however gently, against gravity to perform these simple actions. But in lying down, we succumb to the earth. We stop resisting. We let the world take and hold us.

138

Toward morning, the bed and I have come to an agreement. We each surrender a bit of our control and, as a result, there is a moment, just before rising, when the body is at equipoise with a softness of gravity—almost weightless, balanced on an invisible point, the dawn and gravity.

The night and my frequent adjustments have made my bed my perfect environment. The bed is mine. I find it difficult to break free from this sensuous embrace. If the bed contains another, a loved other, its allure is compounded. Not only are sheets and pillows potential fields of dreams, but the flesh and warmth, the edges, angles, and curves of the other beckon. My body can sense the nearness of the other simply by reading his heat signature. We touch without actually touching, my warmth interfering with the field of his warmth. Feet and hands especially enjoy the proximity of the other inside the warm cavern of the bed, the bed in its most sublime moment—the bed at dawn.

The last moments before rising are the sweetest. They enclose and fit us like tender gloves. And the sheets are accomplices, entwining and binding us even closer in our early morning warmth. The two of us together make it even harder to rouse from this sensory Eden.

Mere chance found me lingering in bed on this morning when the frogs and the blackbirds filled the air with sound. Just think, this happens every morning whether I take the time to notice or not. I always listen closely to catch their ecstatic noises, even if I'm leaping out of bed and rushing to shower, breakfast, and work. I'm changed. The unexpected beauty of morning songs has fused forever with dawn and the warm pleasure of the bed.

139

28

Climbing
Amboy Crater

We had driven to Amboy Crater near the Nevada border in the late afternoon, my brand-new sweetheart, Jack, and I. We were crazy in love and filled with the headstrong bravura our love had inspired. We felt invincible and cocky. We were on a mission. We had made a lover's agreement that we would climb the stout pile of glittering sunburned rock, a former volcano now dormant for millennia, and watch the sunset from the top. We were full-grown adults—not exactly fitness fanatics—who were new to the Mojave Desert, but we asked ourselves between kisses, how hard could this be? We weren't even wearing hiking boots, but did that stop us?

Actually, I *was* wearing hiking boots. I was from the West Coast, land of outdoor activities. Jack was a recent transplant from the urban East Coast, land of sidewalks and fashion footwear. He was convinced that his leather wingtips—whose soles lacked any tread whatsoever—would do just fine. A red flag should have popped up, but I wasn't about to argue with my new sweetie.

At 250 feet high, Amboy Crater is a trapezoidal remnant of hot times past. Six thousand years past. Pale purple sand verbena fanned out in all directions from the ancient lava flows. A little trail invited us up and around the collapsed cinder cone. Following the path proved tedious, however, and taking note of the rapidly setting sun, we decided to take a shortcut straight up the side.

Straight up the side! What were we thinking? Only the surface of a glacier is slipperier than loose volcanic gravel. More red flags should have materialized out of the desert air. What we had fantasized as a brisk fifteen-minute walk to the top became a matter of slipping, losing our balance, clutching at the massive outcroppings and loose rocks and then—placing our feet at horizontal angles for better traction—taking a few steps upward. Those city slicker shoes were busy showing off their limitations. Jack spent the first ten minutes sliding down and struggling back up. I didn't do much better, hiking boots or not. The brittle rocks underfoot sounded like pottery thrown against glass. Shattering shards. Jack and the shards were at war. I reluctantly told him I thought we should turn around. The crater would be here another day.

The dismay (was it hurt pride?) on his face was painful. We had to keep going. Cursing, sliding, laughing, we struggled on. It was late May and even though our ascent (that's a laugh, we were practically crawling up the last fifty feet) took place on the shaded face of the crater, it was hot. We were out of breath, sweating, and my feet were throbbing.

Finally we made it to the top. The surface looked like the surface of Mars painted a horror film shade of green. So baked by the sun was this terrestrial crater it had cracked and buckled into curls of chartreuse pottery. Our footsteps echoed as we pressed on toward the rim that faced west and overlooked the flat Mojave stretched out on all sides. To one side lay the white salt flats, undulating in the heat. Straight ahead was the tangerine sun, growing flatter as it sank into the horizon, turning the sand and surrounding alluvial fans to momentary vermilion before it winked and disappeared right before our eyes. We sighed one single sigh of satisfaction. With the aid of neither common sense nor proper footwear we had done it—together.

We took the more sensible way back down, but quickly, since the light was fading fast. (We had brought neither water nor flashlight.) The temperature was dropping fast, too. Stars began to poke through the indigo atmosphere. We could hear the rocks cool. The shimmering, radiant heat was all but gone by the time we reached the car, drove a dozen more miles to Roy's Motel on Route 66 where we insisted on paying for the only room with sheets on the bed, dined on red wine and pretzels, and dreamed through the night in each other's arms.

That sunset at Amboy Crater carved itself into our aching thighs and ensuing years of passionate kisses. We treasured our love even more for having done that together, that slip-sliding and just possibly semi-dangerous (and arguably stupid) climb to the crater rim to watch a sunset that did what all sunsets do: marked the momentary eternity between day and night. The desert was ours forever from that tangerine moment. It marked the official beginning of our life together.

29

Winds of March

The wind started up every March in the Central Valley east of San Francisco where I spent my graduate school years at UC Davis. An epic wind, a wind of sirocco proportions. It began suddenly, gripping the trees, my hair, and bits of loose paper, and would proceed to shake, rattle, and then shake some more for days on end. The gusts were strong as wild animals, insistent and implacable. Even when I fled indoors to escape the unnerving blasts of harsh, dry wind, I still felt it. It gnawed its way into my brain. The windows chattered interminably, doors banged against thresholds. The trees outside shivered by day, and howled by night. How I hated that wind.

The March winds affected me so powerfully I was unable to finish assignments. I borrowed my roommate's car and drove to the coast to visit a friend as fast as was legal. Intending to escape the maddening winds, I was aghast to discover they had followed me to the edge of the land. There I was in a completely different geography, one sheltered on the east side by high mountains and thick wooded foothills. The ocean lay on the other side. Yet the winds of March were here.

"Don't you just love the March breezes?" my girlfriend gushed as she took my backpack into her house. It took me a minute to realize that she was serious. What was going on here? I was in a big hurry to escape the very weather she was praising. "Explain, please," I asked her. Perhaps she could help me find another way of dealing with the winds.

"Think of the wind as air coming to life," she urged me. "We live with this oxygen and nitrogen atmosphere all the time, but it stays in the background. Air tends to stay still. We know it's there but no one notices it." Right. And?

"When the winds come up every spring—and they seem to do it everywhere there's a Mediterranean climate," she continued, "we can see and feel—and hear!—the usually mild-mannered, invisible element."

We looked at each other. I looked out the window at the trees swaying in the wind. We both laughed. Leaping up from her chair, my friend went to the front door and opened it. We stood on the porch listening to the rustling sighs and shimmers of the wind pushing against a stand of eucalyptus trees. Its unique voice sounded like music. The winds were trying to tell me it was spring. I just hadn't been listening.

Spring comes far more gently and curiously to the house where I live today. We started noticing that tufts of straw fibers had been pulled out of the doormat at our front door. Were we scuffing it off with our boots? Had the neighbor's cat clawed it into messy pieces? None of the above. We caught the culprits one day—a pair of scrub jays busy tearing out bits of soft fiber to carry off into the trees. They were building their nest. Spring announced itself right at our doorstep.

your
turn

How does spring announce itself where you live? Is it loud and showy or soft and mild? What are the sensations felt in your body during the first days of autumn? Of winter?

Seeing the Colors

I once lived in a house near the Sacramento Delta whose weedy backyard contained several flourishing fruit trees. In the heat of early summer, I would stand out under those fruit trees in my underwear and eat warm apricots until I was cross-eyed. The backyard had an old wooden table I had painted cobalt blue. When one of my fellow graduate students came over for lunch one day, I picked a dozen velvety apricots and placed them in a bowl on the table for her to enjoy. I can still feel the visual perfection of the ripe, golden fruit against the intense blue of the table. The colors sizzled against each other in the hundred-degree sun.

The eyes live for color. If I stopped whatever task I was engaged in and simply let my eyes explore whatever they liked, the enchantment would never end. My eyes graze on the colors, shapes, and movements of the visual world as if it were a patterned rug inviting me to explore every dimension. Eyes were made to soak up the world, and the flirtatious world takes full advantage of the eyes' desire. Go ahead. Open your eyes. What do you see?

My office for many years adjoined a tiny courtyard inset with a triangular koi pond. Each day as I walked by the pond, it came alive and bubbled with flashes of orange. The bottom of the pool was dark, so the large orange and gold koi were easily visible. They cruised along the bottom like sleek torpedoes, or floated up to the top to gaze at passersby. I would sit at the wide edge of the pool, between a bronze sculpture and a row of muscular agapanthus. The minute I sat down, the monstrous beauties would swim up to me. The fish loved the attention. I'm not sure who enjoyed the show more, them or me. The sight of these two-feet-long fish, scales glittering, floating and darting, gliding and begging for food, was hypnotic.

149

The patriarch of the pond was a huge blue-black creature with soft eyes and a perpetually open mouth. He would make insistent kissing motions with his lips, his great body framed by delicate fins. Even though the pond keeper frowned upon it, I loved to touch the koi, rewarding them with raisins or bits of oatmeal cookie. I don't regret transgressing. The beautiful creatures from a watery planet were as sweet to watch as waves in the sea. The feel of their slippery heads was an unexpected pleasure for my hands.

Who can resist the mesmerizing effect of flames dancing, flickering, zigzagging from orange to red to purple along a pyre of logs burning in a fireplace or in a campfire on the beach? Flames are alive and unpredictable. They don't tell us what they're going to do next. That's part of the allure. I would love to be a flame, to live as a fire does, burning brightly. When I light a fire in early winter, I'm doing it as much for the visual enchantment of flames and glowing coals going through their endless transformations, as to warm the house.

At the Jersey Shore on a recent September afternoon, I went out to walk along the wide sand, watching the horizon for fishing boats. At the very edge of the sea I saw a row of pale pink clouds, tightly clustered into a scalloped row. Several times that day I returned to watch the progress of the cloudbank as it rose higher in the sky, gathering volume and rosy hue. The clouds bulged; the moisture pressed against my eyes. My eyes were watching a storm brewing, that's what the tall clouds foretold. By sunset the clouds had thickened into lofty knots of crimson and purple. My eyes were spellbound.

When I decided I had a favorite color (though I can scarcely believe it today, it was *purple*), I filled my life with it. I dressed in purple, painted my bedroom purple, wrote letters in purple ink. I was giving a gift to my eyes. And when my eyes wearied of purple—which took roughly one year—I fed them new colors. Now they love to look at red: red sunsets, rosy finches, garnet earrings, strawberries, cherry gelato. The older I become, the more omnivorous my ocular appetite.

Jack took me to Paris for New Year's during our first year together. With so many visual feasts in that great city, one moment took my breath away. It was an afternoon in the jewel-box interior of St. Chapelle. The diminutive Gothic chapel, tucked away in the shadow of mighty Notre Dame cathedral, repaid us handsomely for the half-hour wait for admission. We walked through the ground floor of the twelfth-century church and climbed the stone staircase to the upper sanctuary. The low afternoon sun cast its light directly through a wall of stained glass, making colored patterns on the ancient stone floor.

"Look!" Jack cried, holding up his hand. There on his palm was a rich tattoo of colored light, caused by the sun slanting through an ancient lens of amber, scarlet, and lapis lazuli glass. I looked up and realized that not only was the light throwing rainbows of color on all the people gathered inside the chamber, the air in the room was alive with glowing color.

My eyes are always refreshed by the green of meadows, forests, and trees. They follow the flight of a resident blue jay, taking pleasure in the shock of indigo blue feathers soaring and weaving through the green lattice of sycamore branches. Blue feathers against green leaves, delicious. When I'm working at home the pond outside my window offers my eyes an infinity of greens, depending on the weather, time of day, depth of algae bloom, thickness of cattails and reeds, and the season. Willows at the far edge of the pond can wear hints of dusty turquoise in the winter and brilliant chartreuse in spring. My eyes cherish such abundance.

When a dear old friend suffered a stroke, I went to visit him wearing a special gift. He had been an artist in his youth and loved bold colors. As I went into the room where he lay on his couch, I paused for a moment. I wanted him to see me in my bright pink sweater—a long-sleeved pullover in a shade one could only call shocking pink. I wore that sweater because he had liked it and I hoped the color would lift his spirits. His face changed from frail to vibrant. His eyes actually danced. Only when I approached close enough to give him a hug did his gaze move from the bright pink sweater. Then we looked each other in the eye, while the pink sweater looked on.

151

your
turn

Give your eyes permission to wander. Let your eyes roll over the colors, shapes, and movements of the outside world. Choose a nearby object, anything that catches your eye, and let your mind simply enjoy it. No need to expect anything. See what colors you can discover.

31

Kissing

My first serious kiss occurred by sheer accident. The good-looking lifeguard at the nearby swimming pool happened to be walking to his car as I was walking home. It was a warm, humid twilight, the sky was a dusky purple, and I was filled with the budding hormones of a teenager. He stopped me to say something I cannot recall, and then he asked if I'd ever been kissed. I must have looked clueless, so he decided to be helpful. In the most tender and confident way, he kissed me: a long, deep adult kiss. He was the sweetest of first kissers. And then it was over. Giving me a squeeze and a smile, he walked away into the sultry evening. I remember the feel of his arms around me and the pressure of moonlight on my body. I floated back to my house on a tide of newly awakened desires.

I found myself practicing kissing in the mirror, trying to split my bodily attention into both the kisser and the kissed. It didn't work. So intent was I upon gaining experience in kissing that I organized spin-the-bottle sessions during lunch hours. I would ask some of my friends—mostly boys—to join me. They rarely declined.

My high school boyfriends, however willing to kiss, were mostly amateurs. So I found other ways to make my way into the world of adult kisses. I soaked up feature film romances that offered a wide range of Hollywood-idealized kissing. I could tell if the movie stars were really enjoying the scene. The ones who kept their lips tightly shut, never moving their mouths in the throes of passion; they were simply acting. I kept looking for actual kissing, imagining myself as the woman being caressed and held by a man who knew exactly what he was doing. My favorite movie kisses occurred after much waiting, hemming and hawing, delayed gratification, when finally the two lovers—we already knew they were in love—succumbed and kissed. That moment of tension, the *almost* moment, adds an unbearable heat to the eventual kiss.

The kiss in the rainstorm is my favorite kissing situation. In *The Year of Living Dangerously,* a pair of soon-to-be lovers are caught in the rain, rain drenching their hair, faces, and mouths, and as they finally come together in a fierce kiss, the sky releases its own pent-up passion and the kiss becomes fused with the torrential rainfall. Steamy stuff.

The lover's kiss is the most powerful moment of opening up to another person. The kiss initiates an invisible ceremony of dreams and secrets, a mouth-to-mouth message of desire. Lips touching, lips seeking. They look for response. In kissing, the lips surrender the entire person through eloquent pressure. Lips invite intimacy. A kiss asks for as much as it can get.

A kiss doesn't simply convey desire; it telegraphs information and intention between lovers. I had to admit I was no longer in love with Mr. B when I realized I no longer liked to kiss him. I began to avoid his kisses. When Jack and I first kissed, I felt I'd made contact with some previously invisible force field. Here in the breath of another person was a rush of secrets, a secret language spoken only by the two of us. His first kisses were spectacularly new to me, yet absolutely familiar. Jack's kiss was a homecoming.

Not all kisses are romantic. A kiss can be a greeting or bestow a social benediction. A sudden kiss with a complete stranger can happen at New Year's Eve. I find myself especially moved and empowered by a kiss given just before heading off into an uncertain situation—a kiss for luck. Or the kiss can be a moment of closure and reassurance: a goodnight kiss. The mother's kiss tells the child, *you are loved, go to sleep*. An unexpected kiss from a friend, in the moment of kissing, can become something more. Casual kisses create an undeniable web that can capture just about anyone nearby. Watching a father taking time in the midst of grocery shopping to lean down and kiss his rambunctious child on the top of the head makes me feel warm right down to my toes.

I often stop and admire the sun sinking into the ocean on my favorite walk. All around me, couples walking together seem to fall under the same spell, and succumb then and there to an inevitable kiss. How right they are to be so swept away that my presence, or anyone else's, can be ignored in favor of a kiss. Jack and I find it hard to resist kissing when out walking at our favorite seaside haunts. These kisses seem to be prompted by the setting itself, and when we kiss under the spell of the ocean, it takes on the feel of a ritual. The setting invites us to be more deeply together—the kiss is the symbol as well as the act of being united.

A spontaneous kiss can help put things into perspective, even in an improbable setting, such as when Jack and I stood in front of the toiletries section of our drugstore unable to decide on nail scissors. An impromptu kiss helps to keep us close *(we're in this together)* in the face of a temporarily absurd situation. And quiet, sacred moments of being together, especially when no words are needed, have permeated deep into our shared personal narrative when sealed with a kiss. We kiss to reinforce decisions, to say hello, to round up an event such as breakfast, to say goodnight. Kissing is an ancient farewell ritual. When we love another person, we wouldn't dream of parting without a kiss. Just think of all those train station farewells.

32

The Spell
of the Piano

By the time Frau Lyons came to our house in Wiesbaden to give me my first lesson, I had already fallen under the spell of the piano. When we went visiting, ladies who smelled of lavender whispered to my mother that she really must get me a piano. "She wants to learn, you can see that she already loves the piano." I was five years old.

The moment I first touched a piano, I understood its power. Inside the piano, the music waited. Outside, my hands had to get ready. The piano waited, a mysterious wooden entity, asleep until its curved top was opened and the right touch released its music.

Frau Lyons was a German lady with soft white hair and Old World manners. Her English husband had died years ago and she gave piano lessons to make ends meet. She wore black dresses and had a sweet, encouraging smile. She started me on Mozart, Bach, and Haydn. I wanted to play them all. In addition to the beginner's preludes and sonatas, Frau Lyons presented me with music books of less charm—tall, stern, yellow music books containing not gorgeous melodies or resplendent chords, but homework for the hands, scales and arpeggios. I was expected to work through these exercises, over and over, for at least an hour each day. It was my first lesson in how long an hour can be.

The rewards came slowly, and in direct proportion to the hours I spent on those unappealing scales. Once I grew tall enough for my feet to reach the pedals, I learned the joy of making the fierce chords last. For me, the piano was a boulevard to places of complex ecstasy. When I played Mozart, I could feel that he had been there too, exactly in the place that I was—a place he inhabited and invented in his sonatas. These places can only exist when we play his music. The piano was not only a time machine, it presented the possibility of transformation. As often as I played, I was transported.

When it came time in my studies to move further, into Schubert études, Chopin preludes, and Bartók concertos, the slope of mastery steepened. The results of my practice were not quite as sweeping and beautiful. I would need much more work and dedication to make significant progress. Being carried away at the piano was a far cry from playing with great style and virtuosity. Nonetheless I continued, juggling piano practice with new interests in boys, hairstyles, and writing poetry. I augmented my piano practice by singing with the school's madrigal group, expanding my interest in intricate classical music into vocal performance.

When Frau Lyons retired, I continued on with a new teacher who had many other students. In the back of my mind, I harbored unspoken dreams of performing professionally. At our annual recital, I moved up in the pecking order until I was next to the last on the program, which was almost there, but not quite the top student. Yet that didn't seem to matter. Until it did. After six years of studies, my piano teacher looked me in the eye and told me gravely, "You'll never be a concert pianist."

I was stunned. Was she actually telling me that passion couldn't be converted into expertise? Actually part of me was relieved. Somewhere inside I had known that my affair with the piano was always one of the heart, not of a concert-quality talent. I made a brisk pivot into the world of voice lessons for another year, and then turned my attention to anthropology, fraternity men, and preparation for grad school.

Even so, to this day if I get anywhere near a piano, I cannot resist sitting down for a rendezvous with my childhood heroes, Mozart and friends. Those early melodies are still in my hands, waiting for the piano to play its part. My teacher was right; I was never destined to play the world's great stages. But Mozart is mine forever.

159

your
turn

It's high time you revisited whatever musical practice or pastime you once enjoyed. Sing, play the guitar, do the mambo, harmonize with friends. If you've never tried singing or playing an instrument, take a chance. Join a local chorus, take piano lessons, sing along with your favorite rock star. Stay connected with those joys that bring your body, your curiosity, and the world of music all together.

(33)

Swimming in the Rain

Every summer when I was in my teens, I spent my days lolling on a beach towel laid carefully on the new-mown lawns surrounding the neighborhood swimming pool. I would slather on Bain de Soleil tanning oil, letting its sensuous orange aroma permeate every pore. Just seeing the words "Bain de Soleil" triggers the orangey smell I still equate with summer. The days grew longer, and hotter. I would dip into the pool every now and then to keep my stubbornly pale skin from blistering in the late summer blaze. Then I would stretch out again on the carefully rearranged towel, close my eyes, and drift until my brain began to fry and I needed to cool off in the water all over again.

By August the humidity of our little corner of northern Virginia increased and gathered each day until the sky was as full of moisture as it could get. By three o'clock in the afternoon great slabs of charcoal gray clouds blotted out the horizon, growing darker and darker. Finally, almost black and urgent with need, the clouds gave way. That instant of barometric change from pressure to release was ecstatic. The sky turned to liquid, the rains pounded down, and—if we were lucky—lightning and thunder swelled and boomed from all sides. Those moments were almost sexual in their physical potency. I could feel the gorgeous pressure against my body.

The lifeguard would grab a megaphone and boom in his official voice, "Okay people, everybody out of the pool." The rain plummeted down in huge heavy drops, in sheets so thick I could barely see across the pool. The air turned deep green. Grass, trees, and raindrops seemed to merge into a thick swollen wall.

And, at that exact moment, I would dive into the pool.

Coming back up, I was peppered by the ricochet of rain pounding the surface of the pool. All was liquid—the air, the pool, my body. I was suspended in a tight membrane of water. Buoyed by the chlorine-hued coolness of the swimming pool, my head and hair were drummed and thrummed by warm air and rain. Captured between the two forms of water I was delirious with joy. Rain and pool joined in a liquid kiss with me in the center.

All this voluptuousness never lasted very long, because invariably I would be called sharply out of my sensuous trance. "Out of the pool—and that means *you!*" Surely it wasn't true that I was in danger of being electrocuted? I never got to find out. But with each summer storm, I would try to recapture that joy of submersion and immersion, the mysterious varieties of water.

163

your
turn

We seldom let ourselves stay in a wild place a bit longer than necessary. Just passing through, we never actually get to sample the good stuff. Try lingering with an experience. If you're in a forest, just stay there and wait for things to happen. The animals begin to resume their normal activities. If you stay longer still, the forest will return to itself. Its true personality will resurface—not the quiet, polite attitude it adopts when you simply stroll through.

Let it seep into your pores and deepen your awareness.

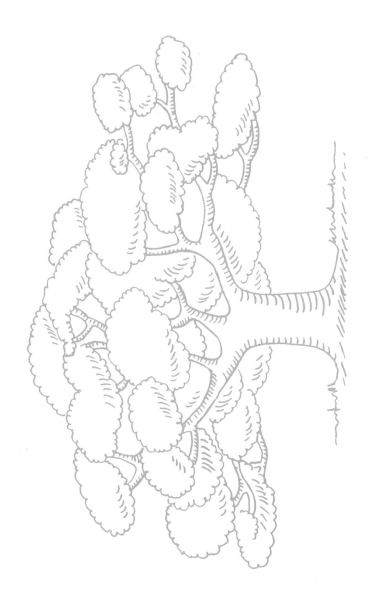

34

Making a Home
Away from Home

In Sartre's early existentialist novel, *Nausea,* his protagonist Roquentin reminisces about a quirky tendency of his old sweetheart Annie, who never traveled without a trunk full of treasured pillows, pictures, and sentimental household objects. As soon as she moved into a new hotel room, Annie would open her trunk and place her personal items around the room, transforming it into a recognizable, reassuring environment, very much like home. Annie loved to travel. She wanted to leave home while bringing it with her. Adorning her new environment was her way of controlling the unfamiliar world.

On a trip to the East Coast, I found myself settling into two new temporary residences: the first, a hotel room in the bustle of Greenwich Village at the edge of Washington Square; the second, a retro seaside motel on the Jersey Shore. In each case I was presented with a small practical space containing a bed, desk, closet, and bathroom.

On my first evening in Greenwich Village, I unpacked, putting clothing into drawers in some semblance of order: underwear in the top drawer along with jewelry and other accessories; pharmaceuticals and makeup in the bathroom; shoes at the bottom of the closet. I emptied out the suitcases and put them away, out of sight. The sight of suitcases can make a room feel transient and temporary. The minute the suitcases disappeared, the room felt less like a camp and more like a residence. Things placed inside drawers created an instant sense of order and calm—and this is crucial, as all travelers know, when dealing with a small space.

Once my shampoo and toothbrush occupy the sink counter in the bathroom, I feel I have begun the invisible process of transforming a generic space into something that has a familiar look and feel. My own blue toothbrush, my favorite brand of toothpaste, these are the everyday attendants of my life. Almost never do I pay attention to these items except when they're missing. In hotel rooms, I find it soothing and necessary to bring the accessories of my daily life along with me. As the days went by, I accumulated a few shopping bags from local stores, each of which added their own bit of color and brand-name character. My favorite notebook by the side of the bed awaited my attention, next to my earrings, watch, and glass of sparkling water. It was beginning to feel right.

The following week, checking into a motel on the Jersey Shore with a large living room and kitchen facilities, I had even more opportunities to reshape essential basic furniture—bed, desk, couch, sink—into a suite of accomplices for my needs and intended activities. A beach chair was stashed in the spacious open closet. Books and notebooks stacked themselves up by the TV remote control. Wineglasses purchased at a local beach mercantile waited on the kitchen counter for the red wine I had bought at a nearby grocery. I was becoming a local.

Within a few days, I had spread out my watercolors and blocks of paper on the end tables, painting in the late afternoons between beach and dinner and spreading the images over the coffee table to dry. The room started filling up with my books, paintings, laptop, and jars of snacks (almonds, crackers, juice). My eyes found increasing evidence of my occupation, mirrored in the idiosyncratic new items and organization of the room.

I'm not like Annie. I don't haul around personal mementos or photos to place around my hotel rooms when I travel. But I do like to visit a local thrift store and find souvenir stemware to use for drinking wine, or retro plates—decorated with World's Fair advertisements or cowboys on horseback—to use for in-room cheese and crackers. I especially treasure the matching Rotary Club anniversary goblets I found in a St. Vincent de Paul store in Point Arena one year. I rarely use them at home, but having them in that motel room gave me an immediate sense of being part of the little town, rather than having to sip out of the soulless plastic cups provided along with the instant coffee next to the TV. I like to bring votive candles with me on trips, and then poke around a few shops to find a glass votive holder: it makes pretty light in the evening and overcomes the bleakness of fluorescent lighting in some off-the-beaten-track establishments.

Perhaps I am a bit like Annie, wanting a new and temporary living space to bear my signature in some way. I am always on a quest for a new space and the new ways it can make me feel. Craving the new, I depend on its familiarity. Bring on the new, I insist. But let it be cozy.

your turn

What makes you feel at home in unfamiliar surroundings? Is there some fetish object you bring with you when you travel? Do something that will help you feel at home in a foreign place. Buy something made locally. Eat a meal made from local ingredients. Spend some time in a park that local residents frequent.

35

Gifting

Last time I had lunch with my friend Lita, she asked me whether I had found the key to that frustrating magazine article on jazz music and Creole spices I'd been writing. She'd remembered the exact subject and my exact difficulties—even though we hadn't talked for two months. But that's Lita. Then she reached into her pocket and produced a lumpy object covered with a folded purple paper napkin. Inside the napkin were two of the strangest things I'd ever seen.

"Can you guess what they are?" she teased. No, I could not. She put me out of my suspense. "Remember those beautiful shark's eggs you brought me from the Atlantic last year?"

I did remember. Odd, hand-foraged from the beach, and utterly incomprehensible in their almost extraterrestrial design, the shark's eggs had seemed perfect for Lita.

"Well, these seemed like the right response," she said.

The peculiar objects were water chestnut seeds Lita had found in Tibet on one of her retreats. Water chestnuts encased in shiny black shells, with sharp cones on one end. They were exactly the right botanical rhyme for the equally weird shark's eggs I'd given her.

A young chef I was writing about gave me a large yellow tomato at the end of our interview. For a moment I thought he was flirting with me. But he was offering me a piece of his mind. David had grown that tomato in his own backyard. It was fresh, organic, and as visually stimulating as his kitchen, a creative workshop where he inspired those around him to try out their wildest flavor ideas until a moment of genius emerged on the plate. I can never see a yellow tomato anymore without thinking of David and the hard work in the garden that helped launch his now-famous organic menus. Yellow tomatoes have become a kind of symbol to me, and not simply of inspiring creativity. The sight of one prompts a recurring echo of that simple but innovative gift. Whenever I dine at David's restaurant I try to go during the peak of tomato season, in the hopes one of those splendid yellow orbs will make an appearance on my plate.

173

I know some brilliant gift givers; people who sense exactly how some unusual or unexpected item will produce a resonance for the recipient. The gifts I most treasure are those that echo the heart of both giver and giftee. A brilliant gift is more than simply the movement of one object from one person to another; it can also be a recurring theme between two people. The gift influences and deepens our bond, and inevitably teaches us something about the giver.

Lacking disposable income to go out and purchase something for my birthday, Anna surprised me with a handmade lavender sachet, a fragrant pillow of patchwork velvets filled with lavender she had harvested. The gift was a winner in so many ways. It was made by her hands and reflected our shared passion for wildcrafted items. The sachet still perfumes the drawer where I keep camisoles and special lingerie. Every time I open the drawer, the aroma continues her gift.

When I was a young wife living in the woods far from home, my new friend Lucinda came over to welcome me to the neighborhood. She brought with her a branch from a fir tree laden with a thick frosting of moss.

"To adorn your hearth," she said with a smile. The branch, with its covering of fresh green, sat above my fireplace, helping me to make friends with the forest I now lived within. Simple and sensitive, the gift was an extension of this welcoming woman.

What a contrast with another gift experience, when a man I'd recently met gave me an expensive sweater—in the wrong size and wrong color.

"All women love cashmere," he said confidently. Well, no. I wasn't just any woman; I was a specific individual. His attempt to impress me overlooked any actual attentiveness to who I was. The gift told me everything I needed to know about why I would not be seeing this man again.

Lita has always been an intuitive gift-giver, once taking the tomatoes I'd given her and turning them into chutney for me. We spent one lunch arguing about the wisdom of eating a plateful of garlicky pasta before going back to work. That weekend when I visited Lita at her home, she thrust two bulbs of "the best organic garlic I've ever tasted" into my hands. They sat on my lap as I drove home fantasizing about a ratatouille I would make that night.

As a teenager living on the East Coast, I eagerly awaited the annual Christmas package that would arrive from my aunt and uncle in California. And it wasn't just because I relished the sight of my aunt's extraordinary calligraphy shaping our name and address on the outside of the box. As we tore open the outer wrapping we were always greeted with the nostalgia-producing aromas of redwood branches. My relatives knew we missed California and their home, so they packed our gifts in a nest of resinous, tangy redwood needles. I can smell them now.

When my mother moved to Southern California, her landscape changed drastically.

"I really hate those palm trees," she would complain when we sat out on the patio together.

"But your pepper trees are wonderful," I pointed out. "And all those pungent pink peppercorns!"

It was true: The peppercorns were a rich, pink color, and when crushed between the fingers, released a spicy perfume. That Christmas, a package arrived with hand-lettered instruction on the outside brown paper wrapping: "Open before Christmas!" Happy to oblige, I opened the box. My nose was greeted with the piquant tang of pink peppercorns wafting from the branches cushioning four little gift packages.

When my aunt was in a wheelchair, unable to visit me in a house with many stairs, I painted a little watercolor of the view from my back window—the green pond, the encircling limestone cliffs, and a special sycamore tree that always turned bright red in autumn. The gift was an extension of the world that had been denied to her, and she cherished it.

175

When Jack and I first met over coffee, pretending we weren't falling in love, we gushed about our interests. We were both Capricorns, born in January, among our other shared traits. After many meetings it became clear that much more was drawing us together than simply tales of travel and books we both loved. Then January arrived, and with it, my birthday. We must meet, he insisted. When he gave me a hug and sat down I felt a bit crestfallen. There was no package in his hand. No birthday card. Perhaps, I thought, I had been simply imagining our feelings for each other.

Halfway through coffee, he took something out of his jacket pocket and placed it in my hand. It was a stone, large enough to fill the palm of my hand, embedded with small, red crystals. "Garnets," he said. "In their natural setting. I found it in a stream in Pennsylvania last year. I've been saving it for something important."

That beautiful rock, my Capricorn birthstone glittering with bits of mica and laced with small garnets, sits on my windowsill where I can see it every day. Jack's gift marked the moment when I knew we really were in love.

your
turn

What's the best gift you have ever given to another person? What made it important? Now think of a gift you could give that would surprise and amaze the recipient. Make or find it, and give it to them. No special occasion needed.

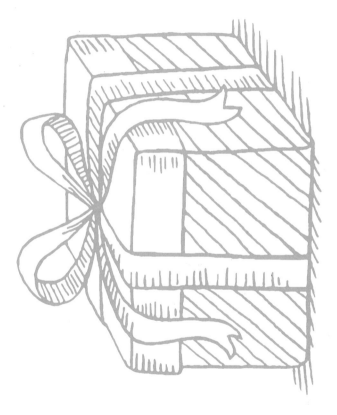

$$\left(\begin{array}{c}36\end{array}\right)$$

The Pleasures (and Dangers) of Touch

Texture is the world's way of getting our attention, of nudging us into a partnership of sensation. Texture is like the value added feature of being born on a planet with vegetation, atmosphere, and climate. I had my satin phase in high school, when everything had to be about smoothness: smooth hair, smooth stockings, smooth suede jackets, and velour pillows.

Then I moved to the rough side of texture. Burlap offered my fingers much more of what winemakers like to call "grip." The small rounded bumps of burlap were like a secret Braille, a language of the fabric holding secrets to its history. Texture is the secret weapon of physical objects. It invites us to reach, touch, over and over again.

My mother made me my first important party dress. It was New Year's Eve, and I was going to a party with my parents. I had forgotten about that favorite winter dress until my hands touched a piece of velvet in a fabric shop. Then it all came back to me. It was chocolate brown velvet, at once sophisticated and sultry. Wearing the dress, touching the bodice and the skirt, was like touching a living substance somewhere between moss and the fur of a cat. It seemed to have its own life, a life I was only borrowing for the evening. Empire-waisted and sleeveless, the dress existed to bring me close to the sumptuous texture of velvet, thick, creamy, and substantial. I wore it as a queen might have worn a ceremonial robe. Think of all the other lovely experiences we compare to velvet: *His voice was like velvet. Her lips, soft as velvet. The velvety evening sky.*

Rough bark reminds my hands how soft and vulnerable they are. Thistles and roses, blackberries and cacti. All of these beautiful creatures prick and poke, tear and cut our flesh. Don't get too close! I once received a surprising gash on my foot, thanks to stepping on a sharp point of broken glass. I burn my fingers nightly on molten pools of candle wax, so seductive in its still liquid but burning-hot state. Texture tells me to stay alert and expect sensations of surprise.

179

I was on a tour of an organic farm one weekend. We wandered through a variety of planted rows of crops bordered by wild hedges of fennel and willow. Pushing aside a pesky green branch, my hand was greeted with a shocking jolt. My finger began to quiver with discomfort. It felt like a jolt of electricity. In a careless moment, I had been approached by a stinging nettle. Intruding into the nettle's territory, my hand was being punished. Back off! My poor hand throbbed not only for the rest of the day, but well into the next one. I was impressed. My hand learned a vivid lesson of humility that day. The hand is not the only inquiring mind in the universe. The stinging nettle has a mind of its own too.

your turn

When your eye catches something, let your body move close enough to touch its surface. Enjoy the unexpected pleasures of sandpaper, dried leaves, babies' feet, smooth rocks. Is there a rare texture experience you've enjoyed? Fabulous! Now find some others.

37

Perfume Tattoos

I can never resist the impulse to reach out for a bay leaf (or is it reaching out to me?) as I enter a certain wood, walking on a certain wilderness trail. After a long procession through open meadows and a few stands of oaks, the edge of the wooded hillside begins. Alternating between great galleries of redwoods and bay trees, the serpentine trail crisscrosses a steep ridge, exactly the sort of ecosystem bay trees love. In warm weather their fragrance is bright, almost thundering. The sharpness of the bay aroma is so intense it seems to assault the eyes and affect the brain. My eyes love to feast on the greenest, newest bay leaves, the small pinky-sized ones at the very tips of the branches. These are the babies, shiny and very lightly scented. But it is the larger, older, and more pungently scented bay leaves that my hands love—demand.

The fingers, with a mind of their own, reach out for exactly the right bay leaf. Once captured, my palm envelops the leaf, squeezing it tightly, and I bring my hand up to my nose to inhale the almost supernatural intensity of the bay scent.

Somewhere along the walk I always seem to lose the leaf. But the aroma has already imprinted my hand. I can simply bring my palm up to my nose and the scent is there in all its glory—a perfume tattoo that belongs, at least for the next hour or so, completely to me.

French Lavender

I was stopped at a traffic light when a man in full bicycle regalia—tight, shiny spandex shorts with matching promotional shirt, aerodynamic mushroom helmet, and clip-on cycling shoes—pulled up next to me. Bordering the sidewalk to his right was a huge bank of lavender in bloom. Few aromas are as distinctive as French lavender, with its tall spikes topped with flames of bright purple that when harvested and dried become the scent of lingerie drawers and body lotions.

I was fascinated by what happened next. The light was still red. The cyclist leaped off his bicycle, knelt down on the sidewalk, gathered some of the lavender flowers in his arms, and buried his head in the perfumed spikes. He remained that way for a long moment, overcome with pleasure. He pulled his head back and then leaned in for more. The lavender was too irresistible. It was an unplanned moment, a chance encounter. But he didn't hesitate; he didn't pass it by. The lavender seduced him from his biking impulse for a time.

183

I smiled at this sidewalk mini-drama, thinking how many times fresh herbs had offered themselves to me as I walked by. Like the cyclist, I was an easy target. My nose is a fool for herbs and spices. The cyclist was my kind of guy, paying attention to the world, not simply cycling through it.

Russian Leather

Whenever my parents went out for the evening, my mother would come in my room and ask me what I thought of her outfit. That's when I would notice the dreamy aroma. She wore the perfume my father loved on her only on these special going-out-at-night occasions. The aroma was captivating and exotic; it was the scent of midnight. Thanks to the perfume, she was no longer my mom, she was a woman embarking on an evening of romance. I can see her in some lovely, close-fitting dress, wearing high heels and a pearl necklace. Her hair, clothes, and scent were all bound up together.

In her later years my mother has given up perfume, claiming she has become overly sensitive to strong aromas. But I claimed her last bottle of Lanvin Russian Leather perfume and now have it safely tucked away. The square bottle, with its original glass stopper, has darkened into a rich amber color thanks to the residue of the perfume. No liquid remains, only the ghost of a fragrance haunts the familiar shape, with its ivory label bordered in black.

Aromas have an uncanny ability to retrieve, or perhaps retain memories. When I remove the stopper and breathe deeply, I stand once again in front of my mother's mirror, watching her put on pearl earrings for a special evening. The aroma is an entire portion of my girlhood, retained within an empty bottle of long-ago disappeared perfume.

Some aromas, potent in their own right, also bear rich emotional attachments. Cigarette smoke reminds me of my Uncle Bud, a handsome, moody man who at all times firmly placed a cigarette between himself and the world. Mesquite smoke invites me into southwest desert evenings and campfires built to warm tea and our spirits at the end of a day's hike. Burning leaves, a scent alas no longer much available, opens a wormhole into my autumns in Falls Church, Virginia, where our neighbors would pile up leaves in the shared cul-de-sac and burn them into pungent ashes. My memory of that place is perfumed by autumn smoke.

your
turn

Kelp on the beach produces a pungent freight of iodine and lean hints of alkaline and soda. Sage, lavender, gasoline, hot coffee, smoke (from incense, burning leaves, or cigars), old-fashioned roses, brandy, and fresh-mowed grass all make my nose happy. Spend fifteen minutes noticing the smells around you. What makes your nose happy?

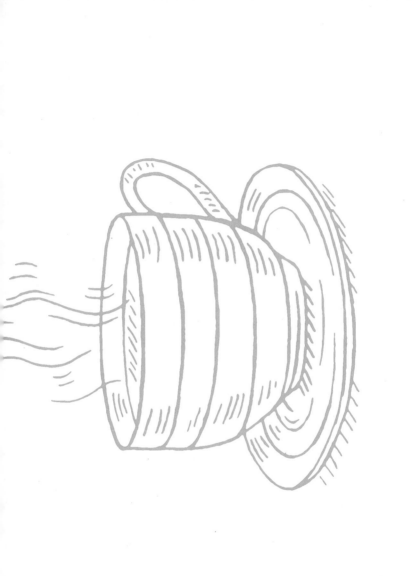

38

Dealing with Discomfort

Lying in the MRI tube, I started to count backward from a hundred in Italian. *"Novantanove, novant'otto, novantasette."* I was going to have to endure the ordeal of this huge, uncompromising, loud instrument of torture for at least forty minutes. Must divert my attention; think of something, anything else. I must not allow my imagination to reach up a mere inch and realize I am trapped in a tight computerized coffin.

My feeling of panic in the MRI was a version of those horror film scenes in which the hero finds herself trapped in an elevator. Only it isn't a normal elevator, it's an elevator in which the walls, ceiling, and floor begin to move inward very slowly. Bit by bit, the sides of the container close in on our movie character, and if she can't figure out some way to stop the process, she will be crushed to death before our very eyes. The MRI felt the same way, like impending doom about to collapse upon me.

The MRI tube didn't actually want to close in and crush me. But I couldn't help the feeling that I was indeed trapped in something much larger and more sinister than most other spaces I inhabit. I have friends who experience the same sense of anxious foreboding with any confinement in a close space. Elevators, caves, and closets can produce a sense of claustrophobia in many of us. Strapped down in the MRI tube I felt overwhelmed by a situation I could not control. The sensation of a dark cave, in which our body fits just a bit too tightly, sets the wheels of a hyperactive imagination turning. What if I get stuck halfway through the cave? What if it doesn't lead anywhere and I arrive at a dead-end, a sudden blockage, and have to try to inch my way all the way back to the opening? Worse still is when we begin imagining just how far below the surface we are. The cave might be one of those passages deep underground, with millions of tons of rock just above our heads. What if there's an earthquake and the rocks start to tumble and I'm crushed?

It sounds like kid's stuff, the anxieties of horror stories whispered in darkened bedrooms. But those imagined fears can carry weight well into our adult years. Sure, you can simply avoid elevators for the rest of your life. Take the stairs. Same thing with caves; no one is forcing you to strap on spelunking gear and climb down into a dark, deep hole in the ground. But many of life's fear-inducing activities can be necessary. Getting a tetanus shot. Going to the dentist. Having an MRI test. When I am forced into a temporary place of discomfort, I call on the aid of a few tried and true coping mechanisms. What can put me in the same state of comfort as sitting on my couch reading a book or walking along the beach? The first time I had to have blood drawn, my mother told me to think of something I liked, a favorite doll or movie character. I found that simply looking at something else in the room, turning my attention to something other than the needle in my arm, helped keep me calm.

Still, that's not always enough. I had to come up with some distraction that was soothing and at the same time would hold my attention firmly enough so it didn't wander. Counting backward from a hundred in Italian provides enough distraction to keep me relaxed in panicky situations. The sound of the beautiful words in my mind keeps me interested: *cinquanta tre,*

cinquanta due, cinquant'uno, cinquanta. Then on to forty-nine—
quaranta nove.

The trick to this diversionary technique is that I am far from fluent in Italian. I can order a meal and find a bathroom in Italy, but the mysteries of the beautiful vowels and tricky grammar still elude me. So the exercise requires all my concentration. If I get lost—and this is very important—I must start over all the way from *cento*—one hundred—and work my way back down. I've discovered this mental exercise will get me through the uncomfortable situation with my sanity intact.

190

your turn

Next time you're at the dentist's office, or in some other uncomfortable situation, try counting backward in some language other than your own. If that's not available to you, recite a piece of poetry, the lyrics to a song, or invent a recipe in your head.

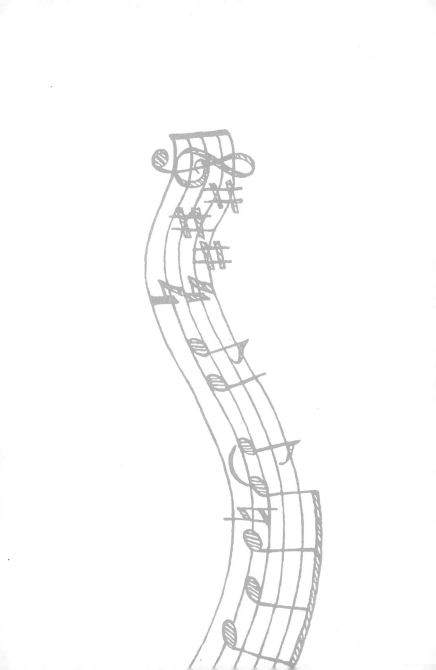

39

Freestyle
Craftiness

Lavonne was an unremarkable person, in appearance. Neat and organized, she looked exactly like the reference library desk and surrounding encyclopedias that formed her workplace domain. She had a maternal face that had probably never worn any makeup and long brown hair that had never been tinted or bleached. Her smile was her most visible adornment, and she made me feel good to be there in my otherwise routine job as reference library assistant.

Lavonne lived alone in an old Victorian house that had long ago been portioned into apartments. She loved to entertain, and one memorable weekend we were all invited—the eight of us who worked with her at the university library—to come over for tea and dessert. I brought some cookies, which turned out to be unnecessary since Lavonne was a cupcake queen and had already set out several varieties of beautifully frosted and decorated little cakes on her antique sideboard.

But first, the tour. Lavonne knew that once we set foot inside the high-ceilinged old painted lady, we would want to poke around the various levels, the antique-laden kitchen, and the small warren of interlocking rooms. I found myself noticing the many needlepoint pillows and throw blankets casually decorating the armchairs and couches. They were unusual, jewel-like textiles with inventive color patterns. By the time we entered Lavonne's bedroom, with both bed and loveseat covered with afghans, I knew that Lavonne had another life as the creator of these vibrant textiles.

"I am a crocheting maniac," she confessed, laughing. But it wasn't only that she made so many of them or that they were so beautiful. What was remarkable about these crocheted masterpieces was that they followed nothing that could be called a set pattern. "I just make it up as I go," she said, offering me an afghan to hold.

195

My hands and eyes said "wow" at the same time. The crocheted fabric was made up entirely of free-form spirals; whorls, huge circular shapes that attached themselves to other, smaller offshoots. Each yarn segment had been allowed to go its own way, and then a new color of yarn would be attached and allowed to fill in and on and on until a bed- or couch-sized art nouveau creation had emerged.

I, who had groped my way through the culturally prescribed handcrafts and even managed to finish a few wearable rectangular scarves, had never encountered anything so astonishing, imaginative, and original. Freestyle crochet. She hadn't asked anyone's permission. She had just started doing it. Lavonne pointed to a small section of blue. "I started crocheting here and when I ran out of that yarn, I attached another color and began working it in a different stitch. Eventually the piece just grew into the size I wanted." With each new attempt, she got better at attaching the sections in ever more appealing and clever ways. Indeed, the more recent afghans had advanced into wildly intricate three-dimensional shapes curving around each other and gliding off into brilliantly hued digressions. Lavonne had invented an entire genre of making something by hand, weaving entire new worlds with only odd pieces of yarn and a number 10 crochet hook. I felt like I'd downed two glasses of champagne—fast.

I mentally tore up every rulebook I'd ever owned after that afternoon at Lavonne's. I began to dig into the world of the made-by-hand with new relish. If crocheting could, in the right hands, become an adventure sport, so could anything I might do or make. That was a rule I decided would fit nicely into whatever I did next: the rule that you don't require rules. You can learn from others, but you don't have to follow them exactly to the letter. Handcrafts would never be the same! Color possibilities grew brighter from that day on.

your
turn

Tackle a creative project without following a plan, recipe, or set of instructions. Just freestyle it. If you use a wildly improbable color thread, or add your favorite fruit ingredient, or paint the exterior of your bookcase bright orange, make sure it's something no one would have expected. Especially you.

"Let's pretend there's a way of getting through into it, somehow, Kitty. Let's pretend the glass has got all soft like gauze, so that we can get through. Why, it's turning into a sort of mist now, I declare! It'll be easy enough to get through."

—Lewis Carroll, *Through the Looking-Glass*

40

Visual Intimacy: Mirrors

I have always been enthralled by the possibility of other worlds existing behind mirrors. As a kid, I often tried to figure out how I could crawl through the surface of the mirror into another reversed world, like Alice did. Reflected in a mirror, the space we perceive unfurls into a much larger space, which is why so many small rooms are equipped with reflective surfaces. The illusion that we can create more space, or at least another portion of spatial reality by means of mirrors, is one that continues to permeate my adult imagination.

I discovered something incredible about mirrors when I was quite small. While washing my hands in a ladies room in an old hotel that had rows of mirrors on facing walls, I looked up into the mirror in front of me and saw myself reflected in it. But it wasn't just a single reflection. As I raised my arms, a hundred pairs of arms raised themselves in reply. I kept peering into the mirror to see where the many "me's" led, but try as I might I could never catch the very end of the procession of images that seemed to curve back into infinity.

We've all done this as kids, and somehow it never fails to delight, this trick of the two mirrors with our body sandwiched between. They multiply the images on and on, suggesting an infinite progression. Thanks to the mirrors, the space in which we live seems to expand into unseen realms.

Mirrors have power amounting to magic. Think about the ability of a single lamp to grow bright enough to be seen by ships far out at sea. It's not done with smoke and mirrors, but by mirrors alone. The lamp's light is reflected over and over into many times the power of its own individual light. And it's done thanks to carefully placed mirrors.

202

I confess to as much apprehension as curiosity about mirrors. Especially distorting mirrors, convex ones that bend light and appear to let us see around corners. My conflicted relationship with mirrors today stems from an experience with a parabolic mirror at a fair. I must have been around sixteen years old. As I approached the round surface, I watched my own body come closer and closer and my features grow larger and larger. My body began to bulge and expand and by the time I was a few inches away from the center of the mirror I realized—to my horror—that I was looking at a three-foot distortion of my own eye. My eye was enlarged and magnified in fish-eye fashion into some monstrous, terrifying part of me. It was me yet it wasn't me. Enlarged almost out of recognition, the eye had become an alien monster, a swollen mockery of my actual flesh.

Why was it so disturbing? Because it represented a version of my body I couldn't recognize as me. It showed my flesh as completely objectified: strange, foreign, and unrecognizable. I have never been able to look at a parabolic mirror again. I know what is waiting for me there: a me grown into something strange.

Creepy as it was, the encounter with the parabolic mirror was highly illuminating. I was not an exterior of grotesque flesh. I was not reducible to a certain height, weight, age, or place in the universe. I was something more, beyond a distorted body. The distorting mirror mocked my inner awareness of who I was. It showed something that others might be able to see, and judge.

But it failed to reflect *me.*

Mirrors tease our myths about our corporeal selves. I didn't see that wrinkle under my left eye yesterday. Or (in a full-length mirror) I never realized how short I was! The mirror delivers us fully present to our own eyes but only if we choose to observe our bodies as an object, like a chair or a table. Our inner sense of self, of course, remains fugitive. The real me is not just some bit of flesh captured in a silver-coated piece of glass.

203

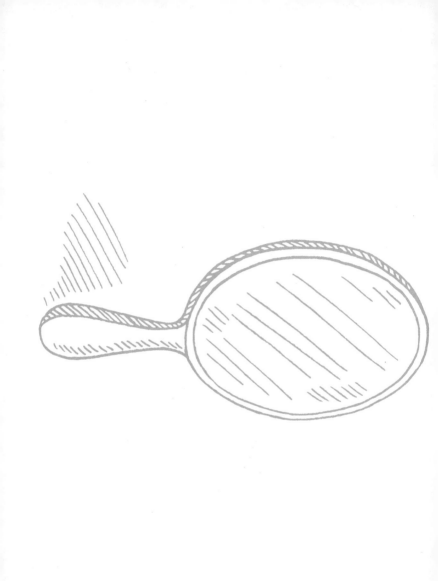

your
turn

Next time you're in a hallway or restroom that offers opposite-facing mirrors, grab the opportunity to wave your arms up and down. Enjoy the sight of your hundreds of pairs of arms waving into infinity. Go ahead and laugh.

When the World Touches Back

Reaching out to pick a flower, feel a smooth boulder, or leave our footprints in the snow is all part of getting to know how we fit into the world. We ask a question; the world provides an answer. The adventure shifts into another gear when the world touches us back—when the world seems to be exploring us. If we're lucky, it happens in juicy, unexpected, and wonderful ways. If we're unlucky, the world can surprise us with its audacity.

The Mystery of Toxic Snow
As someone to whom the roll of the DNA dice gave sensitivity to poison oak and poison ivy—"leaflets three, let them be!"—I learned early and often just how miserably my body reacted to the potent oils of these plants. The itchy rash isn't life-threatening, but anyone who has wandered cluelessly into a patch of these shiny leaves and next day burst into a mass of irritated skin tissue would argue that few physical states are as uncomfortable. While the rash is at its worst—red, oozing, almost unbearably itchy—it feels as though your life has come to a stop. So from a tender age I was vigilant about avoiding poison ivy (on the East Coast) and poison oak (on the West Coast). That meant no cross-country foraging through anything that looked like a mass of shrubs.

After a particularly abundant snowfall in northern Virginia one winter when I was a teenager, I set out to see whether the slender stream that ran through my favorite woods had frozen over. Bundled up in boots, jacket, gloves, hat, and scarf I was well protected from the cold and ready for an outdoor trek. It was the dead of winter. Deep snowbanks, dry remnants of plants and shrubs stripped of their summer foliage—absolutely nothing green was visible except for a few stands of pine trees. I trudged downhill along a familiar trail barely detectable through the deep snow, and had my guesses confirmed. The stream was frozen over. I could glimpse the liquid magic of the water still flowing and bubbling under the surface of ice.

Back home, exhausted by the chore of walking through deep snow, I got warm, had dinner with my family, and went to bed. The next day I awoke with an uneasy sensation. My face felt flushed, and as the hours passed, the flush turned into an unmistakable rash. I was showing all the signs of a raging case of poison ivy. How could this be? After a few days of agony I figured out what must have happened.

Bare branches of poison ivy had been poking through the snow and I must have brushed against them and then touched my face. Even in the dead of winter, the dormant branches were still loaded with toxic sap, and potent enough to turn the only exposed portion of my body into a battleground of histaminic reaction. It kept me out of school and sent me to the doctor for a shot of steroids. It remains one of those indelible life lessons about the dominance of nature's biochemical tricks and the folly of trying to work around its power.

Jumping Cholla

I love the weird contours of cactus plants—their elegant sprightliness and aggressive spikes. I have had a prickly pear cactus named Lester for over twenty years, and his annual flowering continues to delight me. But Lester is happily domesticated.

Cacti in their wild native element are even more exciting. There are so many varieties, and they are so beautiful when the low desert sun creates coronas of light around their assertive armature of barbs and spikes.

However visually arresting they may be, they are still plants with what amounts to an arsenal of needles poking out of their sculptural bodies. The cactus is an inquisitive plant. It wants to learn more about human bodies. Just brush by one accidentally, and you might find yourself either scratched to the point of bleeding, or suffering from the invisible invasion of hairlike cactus barbs embedded in your flesh.

One cholla I met in the Mojave took a fancy to my thigh, and before I realized how close I had come to it, the spike had hit its target. Not just the spike, but also the microscopic hairs along the spine of the cholla branch, each hair with its own barb, quite effective at hooking into flesh (or fur, or hide) and being carried along to new locations. The more I tried to wash off the painful micro-needles, the more they eluded capture. It took a pair of tweezers, one magnifying glass, two adult humans, and three hours to locate and carefully dislodge the mischievous barbs. I forgave the cactus, but never again wore shorts when hiking through the desert.

The world has its own ways of keeping us honest. If you want to head outside of known paths, you better be prepared to take some unexpected consequences. Honoring the limitations of my physical self—getting poison ivy when I am oblivious to its range and tricks, digging cactus spines out of my flesh when my attention wanders—is all part of finding out about the world and how I fit into its joys and its dangers.

your turn

Can you recall your most painful or hazardous encounter with the natural world or one of its creatures? How did you handle it? Could you figure out a better way now?

42

Handwriting:
The Faraway Made Near

A dear friend I've known for thirty years persists in the rare pursuit of writing letters by hand. In response to some discussion we've had over coffee, he will write down a few sentences in reply and I will find in the mail a few days later an envelope bearing his bold and unmistakable hand. Always black fountain pen ink on ivory paper. As I open the letter and read, I feel our bond renewed through the shape of his words. He reaffirms our continued affection in performing this simple act. He has taken the time, the care, and the trouble to take the long way, not the most expedient way. The letters not only convey his thoughts on paper, they convey him to me via the paper. I always (almost always) respond with a written note, sometimes on an antique postcard, or on some special greeting card I've been saving. So far we've been doing this for two decades. And the act of writing the letter tells me that our relationship is alive and well. With letters, it's personal. Beautiful handwriting, usually in ink, usually flowing cursive, was long a highly treasured ability. Before the printing press, it was the only way to share ideas and affections. Old handwritten letters have long been the stuff of family scrapbooks and souvenir chests. Who has not saved a handwritten love letter? Just the formation of the words, the distinctive style can bring back the writer and all he or she means to us.

My handwriting has been part of me for as long as I have been able to write. How I devised it in the first place is something I can't quite remember. Although I confess that I was smitten with the pert vertical shapes of letters written in the fourth grade by auburn-haired Becky McNaughton, who was infinitely cuter, perkier, and more popular than I was, and spoke with a mesmerizing Southern drawl thanks to having been raised in Tuscaloosa, Alabama. I'm sure Becky's unusual and confident handwriting must have inflected my own.

We write invariably from some place deep within our bodies, and that's one of the reasons no typed page will ever pack the emotional punch of a handwritten letter. You can test this easily. I'll bet you've kept a postcard someone sent you from a faraway destination. And I bet what you love about it is that it came to you from some faraway place and you can vividly remember the person who sent it by looking at their handwriting. Not simply the signature, but the actual flow of the words, from their pen, their hand, into yours.

Through the letter we can send ourselves to another. It conveys emotions we cannot express (perhaps because we are far away) or are too shy to say out loud (secret words of secret feelings). By writing letters to a friend or someone we love, we perform a sacred act. We are communicating directly, yet at a distance. Letters also reach far in time—the sight of an old letter with a half-forgotten address and old handwriting takes us back to a long-ago place where all of that still lives. Writing is an act that expands our physical reach, surpasses it, and magically allows us to reach all the way across huge distances to the receiver of the letter. These words carry our feelings, our desires, our thoughts—in essence, ourselves—to another person in another place. And magically, when the other person reads those words, they feel those desires and thoughts. Almost as if we were right there with them.

Several years after my father's death, my mother and I unpacked a box of old books and maps. Sifting through the papers, we both stopped at the sight of my father's handwriting on the outside of a manila envelope. Suddenly he was right there, as if he had walked into the room and was standing next to us while we opened the box. His handwriting brought him back to us, and brought us back to a time in which he still lived. Through the words he wrote, his personality still had the power to move us. Neither my mom nor I experienced that moment with sadness—because he wasn't gone. The handwriting was proof of my father's persistence, of his presence.

I keep the act of handwriting alive in my life by perpetuating a practice that my father enjoyed every year—the ritual of the handwritten Christmas message. It made my father so happy to write to his old friends—those from his hometown, even from high school, as well as those he'd worked with over the years. This annual activity often took him three or four days of effort. I suspect that the receipt of handwritten greetings back to him brought him at least as much pleasure. And it's true that I like to envision the sparkle in my friends' eyes when they see my unmistakable hand on the card they receive during the holidays. Even in the era of electronic communication, I maintain that intimate bit of sympathetic magic—my handwriting, on paper and envelope, sent to them. The act conveys not only my greeting, but my physical presence as well. An embrace across both time and space.

A box of college notebooks offered me something unexpected. I was looking through my old notes on anthropology and world geography. Not very interesting now. But I took some time looking at the notebook marked "Contemporary Philosophy," a bound notebook filled with pale green lined paper. As

I opened it I remembered my fondness, back then, for writing with italic fountain pens. The notebook was filled with my notes on Sartre and Wittgenstein, written in broad letters in black ink. Obviously the work of an italic pen. I laughed at how impractical that little conceit of mine had been. It must have been so laborious taking notes with such a broad-tipped pen, a pen that couldn't move very quickly over the pages.

Then I noticed some scrawls in the margins of the notebook. Not my handwriting—and then it all rushed back to me—my boyfriend's handwriting. My entire body warmed. Here he still was, and so was our young, arduous romance, our habit of writing notes in each other's notebooks during that class. The scrawls in the margin carried him back into my present life. It was only his handwriting but there he was nonetheless. So potent and sweet. My college romance is tucked safely into that notebook, and those sweet years remain accessible, never fully gone.

215

your turn

Think of someone you talk with on the phone or send text messages to. Now sit down and write them a letter. Longhand, on paper. Express something personal using pen and paper. You may find that the act of writing slows down your thoughts, and you say things you might never think to say on the phone, or by email. Now put the handwritten letter into an envelope and mail it. Wait for the surprise and pleasure your unexpected letter produces.

43

A Friday Ritual

"I won't be able to walk on Fridays anymore."

That's what I heard Angela say, but I had trouble comprehending it for a moment. We've been walking every Friday for six years now on a path that skirts the ocean where I live in Northern California. I count on it; I look forward to it. I wasn't prepared to let go of our walking ritual. It was such a part of my week, the last day of the workweek, which found us loaded with work gossip, complaints, movie reviews to share, and a shared love of the superb views of ocean, surfers, and mountains in the distance. My body told me that the ritual walk was important to me. Taking the same walk every week allows me to watch the seasons change in the land around me. I walk for the meditation of it. I walk to let my body feel the air and sky, for my muscles to flex their private language of strength and vigor. I stride through the world hoping to be surprised.

Our walk always starts at the same corner. We head straight for the ocean, about ten blocks in front of us. This part of the walk allows us to check on the progress of plantings, gardens, what's blooming, what's ripening in the yards along the way. Look at all those pears going to waste! Details of the job Angela finds especially oppressing are hashed out and laughed off.

Depending on the weather, one or both of us may shed a layer, wrap a sweater around our waists, or loosen a scarf as we progress through the early Friday evening.

Once we meet up with the sinuous road bordering the coastline, we turn left and begin to accelerate our pace. Surfers might be out showing off flashy techniques worthy of our perusal, and then we slow down, perhaps stop to admire the muscular bodies sculpted by wet suits chopping madly at the waves. We cheer their daring stunts and groan at their occasional flops. And then we move on, past the house we've both agreed we'd like to live in when we are old, a lovely cottage finished with details of rounded rocks and a pretty rose garden perched at the edge of the cliff.

219

If the seaweed has washed up and is steaming in the late afternoon warmth, the smell floats up toward our sidewalk promenade, producing grunts of disgust. We spy a tiny cove where nude sun worshippers lounge and offer themselves for gawking, and we always check to see who is in the buff on a given Friday. There they are—an unlikely yet unmistakable panorama of sun-bronzed, white-haired nude men, looking like Odysseus and his wandering mariners in the Tennyson "Lotos-Eaters" poem, "on the beach like gods together." These men knew how they wanted to live, and they didn't care who else knew it.

When the late summer heat drives locals into the chilly Pacific waves, we take the time to decide who is still able to pull off a bikini. Dogs frolicking are always irresistible as momentary eye candy. We greet friends. I always count on seeing Paul and Peter, who make sure we check them out in their cycling outfits. Renee and Jim, covered up in hats, sunglasses, windbreakers, and gloves are only barely recognizable. Hand-waving all around. There are always a few folks we notice, but would rather avoid, and we often barely miss death and dismemberment by skateboard, bicycle, baby stroller attached to dogs on leash, and often all of the above. "There he is," Angela always whispers and giggles—the guy with the sunburned belly and tattooed arms, trying to stay on a bicycle while being dragged along by his rambunctious German Shepherd.

By the time we reach our turnaround point, established by an unspoken alchemy of tired limbs and impending dinner engagements, we have finished solving my current issues with work and some of our chief gripes about university bureaucracy. Halfway through our seaside promenade, we always perform one more ceremony; at the turnaround point, we reach out our hands to touch the yellow lifeguard box for luck. Then we start back along the cliffs, up the ten blocks (in reverse), and to our waiting cars in the bakery parking lot.

During the fifty-minute walk we've unwound our bodies and tensions, replenished our shared sense of humor, hashed through a few differences—largely about politics and taste in men—and made some future date for dinner or a movie. And, always, confirmation of the next Friday walk.

After Angela's phone call, I was forced to realize how much of a habit our walks have become. More than simply habit, our Friday walks had acquired the force and importance of ritual; a ceremony that costs nothing and achieves a lot. It was the glue reinforcing our friendship.

What was I going to do now? The shape of the week had been ruptured. I felt puzzled, then upset, then depressed. Then, weary of being downcast, I decided to try something else on Friday afternoons. I could sense doors opening as I considered taking a yoga class or using the time for the luxury of reading. I might walk somewhere else, with another friend. I could even walk by myself. The loss of a long-standing ritual didn't have to be fatal. I could create another ritual if I had to. It would simply take some energy, the refusal to pout, and the willingness to dive into some unknowns. Finally I arranged to go over to Dee's house to practice some music. It would be fun—and who knows, it might turn into a regular thing.

But before I could install a new Friday ritual to replace those cliffside walks, the phone rang: it was Angela wanting to know if I could walk the following Friday. I confess I was happy to hear from her, but I had already made other plans.

44

Loss Transformed

"Your aunt is still here," my friend Lita said, in an effort to comfort me. "She's inside you." *Right,* I thought sadly. I was filled with the recent death of a lifelong guide—my aunt, the larger-than-life, intelligent, opinionated woman whose gleaming blue eyes and inquiring voice had been a presence for my entire life. It was true that I could still conjure the sound of her voice in my mind, but I wanted to hear her actual, physical voice. I wanted to pick up the phone and dial the number she'd had for over sixty years.

She died while I was thousands of miles away. By the time I returned, her two sons had taken care of final arrangements and begun taking an inventory of the house and the estate. Lawyers were called, keepsakes had been claimed and removed, and the slow wheels of dividing property were turning in the murky background.

A week later I went to the house, to see the room where she had died. Her eldest son, who lived in the house next door, invited me to look around. I let the force of shock finally enter me, and with it came that disorienting dream state in which familiar objects become unrecognizable. The house, kept much too warm while she lived, was now as cold as a scene from Ingmar Bergman.

I had to suppress the instinctive desire to call out, "Auntie Da, it's me!" and stride into the spacious back room that had become her world during her last decade.

Somewhere in my peripheral vision I noticed the wheelchair, her prison of partial mobility for her last years. The wheelchair was now a mere historic artifact. The stack of magazines and crossword puzzles was missing. In their place were boxes and plastic bags, labeled and stacked for convenient removal. Coin collections. The important jewelry. Family photographs. The leavings of a very long life, the activities, hoarding, and habits. 223

I looked around the rooms of a house that had been my childhood playground and refuge. I remembered all the summers spent here, staying with my cousins during school vacations. The endless barbeques, conversations, ballgames, crazy made-up songs and dances, science experiments, woodworking projects, sewing lessons, cups of coffee, and true confessions. Those moments had long ago entered my body, my molecular structure. They had sprung from a lifetime of encounters with this remarkable woman. I could feel them start to fade, those moments that had fashioned the person I grew up to be—color draining away, energy seeping under the doorways and out through the half-opened windows. Like my aunt, the past with its brilliant images refused my efforts at resuscitation.

I had come to see the old place again, but it was my aunt I sought, with her wildly colored outfits (always decorated with matching jewelry), and her low voice that greeted me in several stages, as if her words arrived from around the corner, starting low and then firing up to full volume. The particular slanting way of opening a phrase, the way she would turn my nickname into two or three syllables as she sidled up dramatically to the point she was about to make. "Hi Teen. Oh! Look at the magazines you've brought."

That was in her later years. In her heyday, her golden age, which seemed to last for most of her life, I would find her at her stove, robustly attacking a recipe, surrounded by delicious aromas. Or she would be in the sewing room Uncle Harold had made for her. Enthroned at her sewing machine, in an enchanted chamber of textile obsession lined floor to ceiling with bolts of fabric, she would show off the new skirt she was making, or a bit of quilted handwork. I can still hear her bracelets jangling as she worked.

In her last decade, the house had been her fort and her shrine. She tended the hearth as well as she could from her wheelchair, resolutely refusing to be pampered or to stop lifting, hauling, and cooking. Until she no longer could. Then the house shrunk to a single back room, the former family room, still equipped with all the paraphernalia of her sons' younger years, walls lined with photographs and insect collections, tables laden with notebooks and reading material, a desk with a computer permanently dealing another round of solitaire.

I fled, stunned by a journey in which I had entered through a familiar, well-worn hallway to find myself in an alien place. I didn't want this foreign land. I wanted her. A month later, on a long-planned visit to another country, I found her again.

As I wandered through a tiny English village, my eye was lured by the sight of handwoven blankets and shawls in the window of a tiny shop. My feet agreed. So I stepped inside to check it out. As my hands sampled the rough, woolly texture and my eyes savored the rich earth tones of a particularly handsome shawl, I heard myself saying, "I wish Auntie Da were here, she would love this." I had this experience several more times. My aunt had a pet lamb when she was a child. I knew she would have loved seeing the brilliant green pastures of the English countryside, dotted with hundreds of woolly sheep. At a village bakery housed in one of those half-timbered relics of Shakespeare's era, the aroma of fresh-baked scones grabbed me. I had to try one. As I bit into its tender warmth I was overcome by the richness of cream flecked with bits of lemon peel and tiny currants. A proper scone eaten on the proper spot in an English village. My aunt, the devoted baker, would have been as thrilled as I was. *Auntie Da, you would absolutely love seeing this, tasting that, being here.* And sure enough, I could hear her voice agreeing with me.

PART THREE

inside the
flame

45

A Well-Made Home

At half-past midlife, my friends Alex and Lee have had their share of troubles. Alex has just finished up a bout of radiation to rid her body of a tumor. Lee's disabled sister spends every summer living in their adjoining guesthouse. One aging parent is stricken with dementia. Yet just stepping through the door of Alex and Lee's house is enough to make me relax. Everything about the home they've made together radiates a sense of joyful vitality. Since they have no children or grandkids, Alex and Lee have poured their everyday passions and lifelong hankerings into their vintage Craftsman bungalow, a treasure trove of welcome for their many friends.

To walk into their home, with its soothing earth-toned walls, vintage wainscoting, and built-in period architectural details, is to sink into a world made by two people who leave very little to chance and mistake. But it's Alex and Lee's experiences, rather than merely their good taste in decorating, that greet me at the threshold. The house records their history. It reflects them and their love for each other. Each wall displays some idiosyncratic bit of artwork or folkloric object collected from their many trips together. Shrines of travel memorabilia seem to sprout in every corner. An antique filigree frame surrounds a circular engraving from a Portuguese antique shop. Photos of Lulu, their oversized Labrador retriever whose golden coat has faded to buttery beige, take up much of the oak hardwood hallway connecting living room and kitchen. Lulu is one of the beloved features of this home—the canine vestal of its hearth.

Lulu's tail wags in time to the soft ticking of an oak grandfather's clock that once belonged to Lee's grandfather (the grandfather's grandfather clock). Liberated from long imprisonment in layers of paint, the early-nineteenth-century timepiece is a gleaming showpiece of Lee's refinishing skills. Over the fireplace, a long wide mantel shows off a collection of round objects, not random, and not overly tidy and fussy. A handsome cluster of spheres made of marble, alabaster, and antique wood form a soothing texture for the eyes and hands.

I couldn't resist asking Lee the secret of their home. She told me, simply, "We wanted a place to come home to, to feel comfortable and yet playful in. We wanted to make it beautiful, yet not too serious." Hence the 150-year-old French bowling ball that sits on the floor at the hearth. You see it there and you think, *Well, of course.*

The pantry gleams with floor-to-ceiling shelves stocked with jams, jellies, and pickles they've made during the last season. Fruit ripens perpetually at the kitchen window, usually citrus or some of the remarkable tomatoes Lee grows in her garden and transforms into jam and chutney. The couple loves to cook together, and manage it without too much arguing, so invariably their homemade condiments find their way into the holiday baskets of lucky friends.

On my last visit, the back gardens were heavy with heirloom tomatoes, fat red bell peppers, and a tree festooned with persimmons. Lee herded me to a seat at the long granite kitchen counter and put a glass of wine into my hand, saying, "There you go dearie." (She always calls me dearie.) It was autumn, and she was deep into the persimmon harvest, making the puddings and dried fruit leather they would enjoy year-round. When she's immersed in her fruit alchemy, Lee's usual uniform of colorful cotton blouses and skinny jeans are discarded in favor of loose khakis and a sweatshirt the exact color of her blue eyes.

"Can I help?" I aimed my remark in the direction of the kitchen, though I knew Lee would shoo me away.

"Just enjoy the wine," Alex said, coming in from the garden with three fat potatoes in her calloused hands. She nodded in the direction of the wine.

"How do you like that Syrah? It's from our first harvest," she said proudly.

Lee and Alex joined a vineyard co-op a few years back and are proudly bottling their own handiwork.

Before I realized where the time went—I tend to let go of mundane pressures like time and appointments when I visit them—the food was on the table. I can still taste the almost indescribable vitality of the freshly dug Yukon Gold potatoes I had for dinner that night at their table. Simply steamed with butter and salt, they made me remember the whole point of growing your own food.

Whenever I am at Alex and Lee's house, I'm convinced that at-homeness is possible. I feel surrounded by the care and regard they feel for each other, and at the same time, welcomed into their life together. I keep trying to put my finger on their secret, on that core reason why being with them feeds my soul. Good friends, friends who can truly invite you in and spend time, create nothing less than a sanctuary. I find myself gravitating toward Alex and Lee's hearth whenever I need some nurturing.

your
turn

My prickly pear cactus, Lester, has been with me for decades. He was the offspring of Lisa Marie, daughter of Elvis, my first cactus. He makes flowers because he knows how I love them. If you have a houseplant you care for, give it a name and regard it as you would a friend. Notice how much more at home you feel. Is it possible that your plants now grow and bloom more vigorously?

46

Ordinary Tools We Love

I have a pair of scissors in every room in my house. One in my bathroom, stuck in the same antique silver pitcher (a memento from my grandmother's childhood) that holds a nail file, tweezers, two large makeup brushes, a dried twig from the sycamore in the backyard, two sticks of incense, and a pen. Three pairs of scissors inhabit my study, including one really sharp pair for cutting fabric. (The study often moonlights as a sewing room.) There are scissors in the garage, scissors next to the downstairs phone, and scissors in the wicker catchall basket that also holds car keys, lip balm, cough drops, postage stamps, emergency earrings, sunglasses, batteries, and hair clips. Kitchen scissors reside in different kitchen drawers. There are scissors at the far end of the dining room table and nail scissors on the coffee table. That's a lot of pairs of scissors, I'll grant you, and each pair is used. A lot.

Holding and cutting paper with scissors is an act my hands have come to love. Scissors endow the hands with special powers—the power to transform and reshape simple substances such as paper, fabric, flowers, and poultry into other more desirable shapes. Scissors feel good in the hand. And they are beautiful bits of engineering, gleaming in their crossed limbs, forming long slender points with two circles at the top when closed and four moving limbs when opened and working.

Tape, glue, hammers, and twine are other common, unsung heroes of everyday life. Our hands love to hold and use them. They extend our reach, increase our ability to make new marks upon the world, complete projects, and attach one thing to another. In the house where Jack and I live, since we often lose items of great usefulness, we have many redundancies of these items: extra scissors, an entire drawer full of tape, twine in the pantry, and glue in the kitchen, garage, and bathroom. Surely everyone does? How did our ancestors live without tape? Putting two things together with tape means that almost any two-dimensional surface, in the twinkling of an eye, can become bigger, longer, more than it was.

Tape is the freestanding sibling to glue, that other bonding sorcerer. Glue makes things stick together. Glue is our comrade in projects requiring attachment, or reattachment, as when we attempt to glue back together a broken cup or plate. Glue helps us collect cards, ticket stubs, letters, and mementos and organize them into scrapbooks. Elmer's, that white oozy stuff that usually gets stuck and hardens at the top of its handy container, requiring lots of poking to reopen the hole, is a sort of private joke among household entities—a sticking agent that gets stuck.

The hammer, a heavy object that fits in the hand and can forcefully pound another object, must be one of the oldest tools in the human arsenal. With its metal head and smooth wooden handle (literally putting the "hand" in "handle"), the hammer cries out to be picked up and put to work. My Uncle Harold taught me that before you hammer nails into lumber of a woodworking project, you must first apply Elmer's glue. Then you hammer in the nails to ensure that not even nuclear attack will sunder the bond between pieces of wood.

Twine belongs to another branch, but is in the same tribe as tape. Twine holds things together, but requires, nay, invites, even more intervention by the hands and fingers. Twine is sensuous and lovely to look at. Unlike glue or tape, it can assume new and intricate shapes. When it becomes rope, it can be tightened into knots that hold objects together. The flexibility of twine, and its big brother rope, puts it into its own niche as far as handiness. Fingers get to do a lot more baroque dancing when they engage with twine and rope, those practical cousins to more decorative thread and yarn.

236

I love using these most ordinary of mundane implements. They provide such appealing ways to solve daily problems, expanding the power of simple actions. Tape, glue, scissors, and twine infinitely amplify our body's ability to make, repair, renovate, and collect things. Life is richer because of their modest contributions, and unthinkable without them.

47

Paper Devotions

Laurel and I share an unreasonable affection for paper. For years we have enjoyed outdoing each other with examples of particularly striking or rare paper. For her last birthday I rummaged through my stash of note cards to find just the right, special card to send her.

Whenever I travel, I like to forage for interesting paper: full sheets, folded cards, envelopes, notebooks, postcards, you name it. I've amassed a stockpile of elegant envelopes, heavy cardstock, unusually tinted writing paper, and embossed note cards—the sorts of special vehicles for greetings that show my regard for the recipient. Stationery stores enthrall me. It's like stepping into a world designed purely for my pleasure. The shelves are packed with rolls and stacks of paper of all kinds, colors, and textures, infusing the shop with the soft, dry fragrance of some faintly woody perfume. It's a scent I have come to know and love only as the smell of paper.

One year my friend made an envelope to accompany her letter to me. The envelope had been lined with marbleized paper, and only when I opened it was its ravishing beauty revealed. I responded with a note on paper with thin gold borders and sent it in an envelope of deep hunter green.

I have many greeting cards of handsome Japanese woodcuts. The colors are crisply outlined by black line-work. The atmospheric backgrounds softly graduate from dark blues into soft lavender hues. The paper itself (even apart from its usefulness) gives me enormous pleasure to touch and to look at. It ripples with raised embossing, and the matching envelopes are just as sumptuous. This is paper that demands to be respected, and requires an appropriate pen. I take extra pains with my handwriting when using this paper. As I write a thought or greeting across the luscious surface, I enjoy the feel of my fountain pen moving in easy loops and curls across the cardstock. Laurel will love receiving this card, I know, because she loves paper the way I do.

238

Paper has colonized every space in my world. I cannot imagine not being able to reach out and grab a notepad or piece of paper on which to jot down a message to myself. My computer wears a perpetual necklace of tiny notes and scribbled reminders. The sticky note is one of my closest confidantes, attachable and easy to keep nearby. My car boasts its own stash of notepads—in the little ledge of the door, in the glove compartment, in my trunk—just in case I need to write down a thought, a grocery list, the name of a song I have just heard on the radio.

I've been in love with paper—its surfaces, its tints, its usefulness—my entire life. Paper is sheer pleasure for the hands; the carrier of thoughts; the bearer of doodles. Entire cultures have been created on its fragile surface, and just as easily lost forever.

In my purse I keep a small, gray Fabriano notebook. This special notebook fits perfectly in my hand. Its heavy pages are large enough to hold complete sentences and ideas, yet not so big that it is unwieldy to hold. My hands love to open this notebook and smooth out the paper before I begin to write. When I open the gray notebook to a random page, I find a small sketch Jack made while we were at a restaurant. Next to it, in green ink, are a few words—"mineral finish, nose of nectarine and citrus"—that belong to a wine I tasted. If I turn back to the very first page, I can read a dream I recorded from the end of the year. I keep these small notebooks stacked up precariously, in chronological order, on the top of a bookcase next to recordings of treasured operas. All these bits of memory form the connective tissue of my history, and thanks to precious paper, they are always within reach.

239

48

Trail of Wild Grasses

Whenever I arrive at a new place or need to emotionally arrive at some new realization, I walk. I've never taken a walk without being thankful that I did. Without a daily walk, my body would start making the kinds of noises cats do when they need to be fed.

I take a certain walk each week in the late afternoon. I usually go alone and let the rhythm of my stride unwind the tensions of the day. The well-worn trail follows a narrow road that once led to a limestone quarry; the road itself was made from a trail established by the native Shoshone many years before. Given the abundant wild creatures I have seen on the trail, I suspect the native peoples used a path that had been blazed by animals before them. The trail threads open meadows that overlook the blue of the ocean and mountains in the distance. Then it plunges into thick forest for a while before emerging in clearings where the rock was quarried in the last century.

On one memorable walk I heard an undulant melody of silvery vibrations—part noise, part music—which I could feel in my chest and throat. I had entered into a corridor of crickets generating a slightly metallic purring. It changed frequency, the oscillations lowered and then sped up again, rising higher in my ears as the path curved toward the woods. The sound appeared to bend as it accompanied the grassy aromas of the open trail, and then dissolved into silence as I entered the shade, where the spice of bay and redwood grew stronger. (My childhood opened up inside me as these aromas thickened.) The rustle of leaves gently filled in the space where the cricket music had been. Far down the hillside, the wind filtered the great stands of ponderosa pine and redwood and the thick banks of tanbark oak and bay.

241

I turned around at a stone labyrinth that is maintained as if by magic by unknown hands, and reentered the sunlit meadow. The light, cushioning corridor of the crickets greeted me again. And I suddenly got it. I had entered *their* world.

The cricket melody was the architect of this landscape as much as the wild oats swaying and bending in the breeze. The sound shaped my walk as much as the temperature did, changing its inflection from the heat of July sun to the cool layer of fog. The pitch of the cricket song rose and fell, deepened, and then—as I rounded a final bend in the path—faded back into the tall grass.

Even the path itself impels me to take this walk according to its history and geology. The path changes as weather (rain, freezing, baking sun) and fellow walkers (dogs, runners, baby strollers) influence its width and surface hardness. The rocks that poke through the soil push insistently against the foot and force me to walk differently, adjusting to expand the path's perimeter. When the trail crosses a spring hidden deep underground, the air becomes cool for a few seconds. Inside the forest my body is greeted with a sudden envelope of warmth. As I reach the rise in the path, the ocean sea breeze rushes toward me. My face is both hot and cool at the same time. The cold/hot of that particular moment of summer evening on the California coast is unique to this place.

I only think I'm in control of where I walk and what I see. The earth herds me in certain directions, and over seasons and centuries those directions have become engraved in the land. Pathways and roads are worn, carved, imprinted. I adjust my footing to match the land's patterns, shaped by weather, animals, and time.

Yet the land wasn't suddenly quiet. The crickets had handed the afternoon off to a covey of worried quail trying to cross the path on my left. A rabbit darted across the trail into the fringe of manzanita. A red-tailed hawk cried overhead. I looked hopefully for the resident bobcat I sometimes see at this point on the trail. He and I have often walked together (on opposite sides of the trail) until he vanishes into a secret ravine. I glanced over to a meadow several hundred feet off the path, the grass dazzling in the setting sunlight, and saw a family of coyotes, a mother and two young pups, frolicking and playing, safe from human walkers and their dogs. I thought of a favorite line from Frank Herbert's science fiction classic *Dune:* "Hope clouds observation." Hoping for a bobcat, I found coyotes.

242

your
turn

Fall in love with a tree. I'm serious. Get close to your immediate world by starting with what you have. A blue jay you've come to know who stops by for a peanut now and then. That big crow who calls out overhead when you step outside the front door. A special tree whose branches pierce the first light of morning, and which holds the last drops of sunset in its crown. Don't be reluctant to greet that tree. It will know you're there, it can sense your care for it. Let it into your emotional ecology.

Musical Homecoming

A few years ago, a friend at the university department where I worked mentioned she had joined the concert choir. This year they were going to perform Mozart's *Requiem*. Would I consider joining the choir to sing with a large orchestra? The thought caused my body to flood with joyful memories.

As a child I had looked forward to choir practice with the sort of hunger some people feel about ball games, holidays, or birthdays. I had actually sung the Mozart piece with my church choir and chamber orchestra when I was thirteen. Yet I felt anxious. Did I still have a voice? Years of red wine with dinner, a stint as a smoker—surely those had taken a toll. Even the passing of time can diminish vocal abilities. For decades I had made excuses for not reuniting with music: I no longer owned a piano; I was too busy with work; I didn't want to risk the deep ache of disappointment. Besides, the university group would be filled with young undergraduates. Would I even fit in?

Still, Mozart beckoned. Mozart was enough to banish many a fear. I knew it would be foolish to resist this stunning opportunity. I finally convinced myself that the joys of singing again would outweigh any embarrassment, and with heart pounding, I went for an audition.

The rehearsal room was filled with young music majors and a few older singers like me from the university community. I had chosen something familiar to sing, a simple piece from the *St. Matthew Passion*. I hadn't sung a serious piece of music for so long. Yet I trusted my skill to be there. My uncertain and wispy start was not promising. Still, I pushed on and my voice started to return, no longer beautiful, but surprisingly sturdy and sure. It wasn't the lovely soprano of my youth, but something slightly deeper in tone, a contralto. In the act of singing, bringing the music to life, I was conscious only of the moment. No worries or anxieties, no obsessing about my mother, credit card bills, or growing older—nothing but the music existed.

When I finished the piece, my hands stopped shaking. Nervously, I looked up. The music director was nodding. "Good," he said, and rose to shake my hand. "We need another mezzo."

Practically levitating with pleasure, I somehow found my way out of the office.

For three months, my new colleagues and I rehearsed long and hard. I had gained a new community of singers who felt the same passion for music that I did. Music was back in my life, like an old friend suddenly writing to me from across the years. The conductor, confident and professional in his tux, took the podium. He smiled his secret knowing smile at us. We all stood on the stage together—together in this special way—and all because we had dared to make this pact. We were ready to bring Mozart's great work of musical art to life. We smiled back at the conductor and took a deep, collective breath. And we sang.

your turn

Did you have a favorite folk song or tune that you learned as a child? Surely you can think of one. Try singing it now. Next time you're at a restaurant and the waiters all sing "Happy Birthday" to one of the patrons, join in the singing. How does it make you feel?

Quilting:
Making Something
from Nothing

Each morning when I get out of bed, my hands caress and admire the details of the quilt it took me a year to make. As my eyes savor the colors, textures, and curved shapes of my handiwork, they can pick out special pieces. The curtains from my first house in the woods. A bit of gorgeous silk my sister had bought for me in San Francisco. The orange-and-white print from a skirt my mother made me when I was a little girl. A Hawaiian shirt I'd made for a long-gone lover. The cocktail gown I'd been so proud of. A piece of mauve silk my girlfriend Dee had donated to my quilt. (I still have the quilt, but my sweet friend Dee died before it was finished.)

Over the years, I saved many beautiful scraps of fabric, most of them taken from clothing worn by me, or those I've loved. Each one is a tissue of memory. I promised myself I would use them one day. And every morning as my hands smooth the patchwork quilt on my bed I can feel my own life story come alive.

I knew when I began the project that I wanted to create a traditional piece of textile work, completely quilted by hand. I also knew I wanted to invent my own pattern, so that the beloved scraps of fabric would be organized according to my own design. The fabric was the key to why I loved making it, and why I love seeing and touching the finished quilt, something of a scrapbook of my life up to this point, saturated with places and people gone by.

I've always liked to sew, thanks to the legacies of my seamstress mother and aunt. Sewing my own clothes meant I could wear fabrics and colors of my choice. It also meant that I had accumulated a stash of leftover pieces from the clothes I'd made. Looking through the fabric pieces, a dominant color scheme began to emerge. Red played a huge part, as did green patterns, turquoise, gold, and yellow. The top of the quilt—the piece upon which I would lay the patchwork squares—was absolutely going to be a buttery yellow. After much fussing and planning, the final decision dealt with the color of the bottom fabric, the part that would rarely be seen since it formed the underside of the entire creation. I perused the fabric shop, and in a burst of recklessness let my hands fondle a bolt of tomato red cotton. I was delighted by the very idea. Tomato red it was. And so I began.

An oversized embroidery frame held the fabric beast I'd assembled while I applied teensy little, eye-watering, hand-cramping stitches to small areas. It took many, many long evenings of handiwork, and the commitment not to give up. When I laid the finished quilt on the bed for the first time, I wept. In front of me was a beautiful object I had brought into being. Not only was it beautiful, it embodied a sensory landscape of my life's history. The little cabin in the woods lies within those ocher paisley curtains. My sister's silk that I'd turned into a luxurious negligee—now its fabric is a part of my waking up and going to sleep. My eye lingers on the square of cotton my mother sewed into a dirndl skirt for my six-year-old self. Surveying the colors of fabrics for clothing I had made, I can see how they changed as my taste changed, and favored new colors and patterns. Thanks to my precious handmade quilt, I curl up each night under a blanket of memories. A warm companion to sweeten my dreams.

your
turn

Make something happen! If you used to sew your own clothing, knit scarves, or build cabinets, why not do it again? Revive that old skill. But even if you've never made something with your hands, you can always make something grow. Plant some flower bulbs in the fall: daffodils, tulips, hyacinths, whatever you like. Savor the magic of transformation!

$$\left(51 \right)$$

Seeing Up Close
and Far Away

My grandfather always kept a magnifying glass on top of his oak dining table. That way it was immediately available when he wanted to examine the fine print in a magazine or newspaper article. Even before he gave me permission to use it, I'd had my eye on that magnifying glass. With a lens four inches in diameter, it had a brass handle discolored by age with a curious turquoise patina. Once I got the hang of how to use this bit of visual sorcery, I loved to examine the world more closely. The lens allowed me to see more detail of the material world by magnifying its complexity, bringing its little furrows, nooks, and crannies closer to me. I took the magnifying glass into all the rooms of my grandfather's rambling Victorian house, peering at the wallpaper, examining illustrations in books, feasting on the new information I could discover in the crocheted lace curtains in the front bedroom. The world just kept expanding and increasing with detail, nuance, and a sense of depth I hadn't realized existed.

I also loved to fool around with its weird image-distorting properties. Hold the lens with its edges toward you, I discovered, and the trees outside appear to warp. If I got my eyes right up to the surface of the glass I could make my hands into long, wavy objects through refractive sorcery. It didn't take me long to see another magical property of perception the lens created. If you looked through it at arm's length, it reversed the world reflected in its polished surface. The looking-glass world I glimpsed through the lens was upside-down, creating puzzling and captivating perspectives my brain loved to grapple with. The lens transformed the world into a place of enchanted impossibilities, of fictional reversals.

I no longer assumed that what I saw with my own eyes was all that was really there. The world had assumed more dimensions, and even if I didn't call upon them all the time, I knew they were there. The magnifying lens gave me access to new realms of my imagination. As I looked I imagined new detail supporting the surface of the world. Those details encouraged my interest, and found their way into paintings I would make and stories I would write. The world was far more intriguing—and larger—than I'd realized.

Discovering the complexity of tiny intricate worlds—ones that waited only to be seen right here in the everyday world all around me—was a continuing source of adventure and inspiration. All the more so the day I put on my sixth-grade girlfriend's glasses, looked out toward the forest, and was dazzled. "You can actually see the leaves on the trees!" I exclaimed. Pretty soon, I too was seeing all those leaves, thanks to my own pair of glasses. This experience renewed my quest to see more of the everyday world through the expanding influence of well-placed lenses.

Magnifying glasses exposed a profusion of sensory minutiae all around me. One day my eyes met a world-expanding lens that exposed the enormity of my extraterrestrial neighbors.

My dad's friend Vince was the owner of a large telescope he'd built himself. A gifted host, Vince often invited his work colleague, my dad, over to visit his home in the Taunus Mountains overlooking the Rhine. Vince was a loud, rotund entrepreneur, always talking, always laughing. He must have had an interesting house and a lovely wife, but all I can remember is his role as sorcerer in my young life.

"Would you like to look through it?" he asked me one night, when my family was over at his house for dinner. He tinkered with a few knobs and buttons, tilted the large round face of the telescope toward the full moon, and invited me to look through the eyepiece.

I was enchanted by what I saw. The round white ball I had known as the moon suddenly took on a glamorous and complex persona. It had subtle tints of pink and green in what I now saw were actual valleys, mountains, and craters crisscrossing its glowing spherical face. I scanned its pale, scarred vastness, following the details to the very edge, where they seemed to fade and then dissolve into shadow. "That's where the light of the sun is being blocked by the Earth's shadow," Vince explained. And with those words, the once disc-like moon expanded into a three-dimensional globe.

When I finally tore myself away from the magical scope, I looked up at the moon with my unaided eyes. There was the old familiar orb, sitting what seemed like a million miles away in a cold black sky. But I knew better. The moon was now a close friend. Vince's telescope had brought the faraway tiny satellite up close and available for my exploration.

I always look for the moon on clear nights, admiring its saucy transformation from elegant little sliver to full-bodied sphere. I rarely look through telescopes these days, but I can still admire the shaded craters and subtle striations that are visible to the naked eye. Inside me I carry the secret knowledge of the many sensory worlds tucked inside, or soaring beyond, the immediate everyday of my senses.

your
turn

Find a pair of binoculars and use them to get a closer look at the moon on the next clear night. Visit an observatory, if you can find one, that lets visitors look through a telescope. Make friends with a magnified universe.

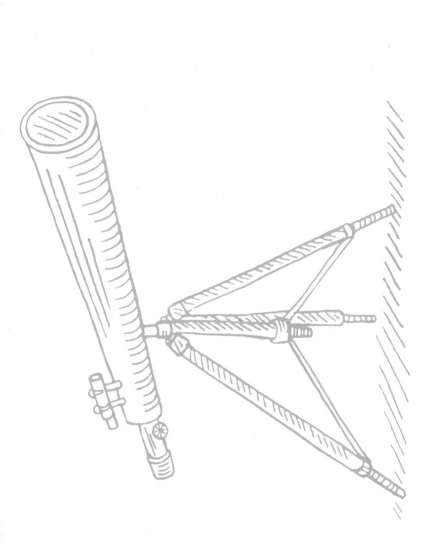

52

Death Valley
Millennium

Jack and I were excited about the upcoming millennium in the last months of 1999. On December twenty-ninth, we set out in a trusty silver blue Honda Civic—my car loves adventures like this—bringing with us lots of New Year's snacks such as roasted almonds, oatmeal cookies, trail mix, a wedge of Fontina cheese and sesame crackers, and some notebooks to sketch and write in as we awaited the hallowed midnight hour.

On New Year's Eve day, we drove through the snow-dusted Panamint Range and then down into Death Valley. Hushed in its vastness, the valley stretched as far as we could see in either direction, contained on both sides by the mauve mountains of California on the west and Nevada on the east. In the fast-lowering sunset light it changed colors every minute, finally agréeing on indigo as we approached a long, deep green mesquite grove that stretches across the lowest part of the Valley, near Badwater.

We had agreed in advance there was to be no communal campground on the special night. Jack liked privacy, and he loved the idea of carving out our own special territory in the vastness of Death Valley. We were going to find our own special place to spend the last night of the old millennium, outdoors under the stars in the lowest point of elevation in the country.

"How about that little outcropping?" I asked. The hill looked like a Martian landscape—it seemed small in the deceptive dimensions of the immense desert—dotted with bits of maroon volcanic rock. Must be iron oxide, we agreed—how exciting. Even though midnight was hours away, we grabbed flashlights and scouted it out. The rocks were sharp and assertive, but the hillside facing the road appeared to be a welcoming and gentle slope of relatively soft sand. We walked back to the car, making a note of the mileage between our millennium spot and the dining room in the Ranch at Furnace Creek, where we planned to get a reasonable meal and while away some time.

Dressed for a summer evening's hike even though it was the end of December, we stretched out our dinner of burgers, fries, and salad for as long as we could, poked around the gift store, bought a few bottles of water and some chocolate, and headed back to the car for our date with history.

We had a digital timer that would help us know exactly when the Hour had arrived. We sat in the car for another two hours, happy to be inside the relative warmth of the trusty Honda. Jack is just a few inches taller than I am, so we both fit neatly into the rather compact front seat. Death Valley was a balmy seventy-five degrees in the afternoon, but the temperature quickly plummeted when the sun went down. Putting on our second layer of sweatshirts and down parkas, we gathered our holiday supplies— emergency almonds, water, that special bottle of champagne, the timer, one sleeping bag, and each other—and left the sanctuary of the car for the appointed party spot in the rugged desert.

Once we settled in the sleeping bag—which was not made for two people (even two relatively small people) and refused to zip completely on one side—we looked up into the forty-minutes- til-midnight sky. I'm quite sure that my fingers had turned blue inside their cotton mittens. But we were humbled by what we saw above us: stars, in numbers so lavish we could practically read by their light. We recognized our favorite constellation Scorpio, the planet Mars, and the Big Dipper low in the sky practically touching the mountaintops. Stars pressed against our eyes, our lips, our hands. We were speechless with enchantment. All of this starlight, so close, powdering the mineral air of the desert. No city lights or passing cars, nothing to obscure all of this transcendent beauty. The millennium scarcely mattered. We gazed and gazed. We kissed, and then we fell asleep.

The cold woke us up a few hours later. I checked my watch. 1:30 am. No! Our timer had failed to go off. The millennium had come and gone.

"I can't believe it," Jack groaned. "I bought that stupid timer just to count down to midnight."

We had missed the moment. One century turned into another while we were fast asleep. Too frozen and tired to open the champagne, we grabbed our gear and walked back to the car. Folding back the front seats as far as they would recline, we dozed until first light, covered by the sleeping bag and the sweatshirts. Then we headed up out of the vast valley as the sun rose on the first day of the bright new year, the year 2000.

We never opened that special bottle of New Year's Eve champagne. To this day it sits in our refrigerator, still encased in its grubby red foil wrapping, a reminder of the night at the end of the century, the night our bodies filled up with stars.

your turn

Ever tried desert camping, or cross-country skiing? As long as you bring some water, a down parka, gloves, and sunscreen, you might find yourself exhilarated by testing such extremes. If you've never slept overnight in the wilderness, give yourself that experience. You'll come away astonished.

53

Diving through
the Wave

The mother was as tall as her two sons. They were speaking German, and my ears recognized the familiar inflections. Someone at the restaurant said they were Austrians, renting a beach house next to our hotel. Mr. B, my longtime newspaper colleague and I, were on a beach on the Mexican Pacific, a sweet little bay encircled by palm and coconut plantations, filled with inquisitive neon fish and baby stingrays. We could feel the fish caress our ankles as we waded out into the pale green waves. Mr. B was a powerful swimmer, and he insisted we make the most of our time in this perfect landscape for swimming. He loved to throw his large body into the warm water, swim far out into the green waves, brush back his blonde curls in a heroic gesture he'd probably seen in the movies, and start back for shore.

Mr. B liked the looks of the three Austrians, too. The mother, statuesque in her black one-piece suit, blonde hair set off by a single gold chain necklace, always led the way out into the water. Her sons, in their early thirties, invariably followed her into the water. They were like mythic characters, tall and strong, and they would dive right in and swim far out into the green water. I loved to watch their strong, steady strokes and their tanned shoulders gleaming with salt and the dazzling heat. All the way out into the tall waves, they would talk and laugh. One of the sons would splash his mother, and she would splash back. They loved the water and they loved each other.

We often followed them into the waves. One of the special pleasures of the sheltered bay was the shallow bottom, so that even I could wade far out into the opalescent surf, my arms covered with shimmering light refracted by sun and waves. I would swim, and then peer down through the surface to admire the neon fish. Mr. B would go further, often standing out where the Austrian trio liked to wait for a nice wave to catch and body surf all the way back to the shore.

I managed to catch rides on some of the smaller waves, but I always joined them rather awkwardly in mid-roll. I kept hesitating, convinced I couldn't go that far out without being flattened by the breaking waves. There was a huge bank of high waves that felt—to me—like a barrier between where I could still stand up easily and the perfect far—but frightening—place at which to catch the wave all the way back to shore.

Every day we would settle ourselves on the beach, positioned under a thatched beach canopy, a rustic *palapa,* where we lay on beach chaises with our towels, sun hats, books, and Mr. B's trusty portable music and headphones. It was hard to stay fixed on a book for very long, so mesmerizing was the water, gently rolling like molten gold. Every hour we abandoned the beach, often at the exact time as the Austrian family, and we would all walk out into the warm water, drawn by unseen forces back into the saltwater of our origins.

Mr. B would continue out beyond the point where the waves broke, positioning himself at a polite distance from, yet somehow in communion with the Austrian swimmers. On the third day, I tried to follow them out to where the good waves were. My strategy was to wait until after a wave passed, and then try to jump up over the top of it and land back down on the far side. But this style of trying to cheat the wave of its power usually backfired. One time it almost defeated me. I jumped up in an effort to get past the wave, but the wave had other plans. I was completely swept off my feet and tumbled like a pebble, head over heels until I managed to claw my way up to the surface, panting for air, shaken and scared.

The waves were always going to be able to toss me off my feet, I realized. So I stayed on the shore side of the break, enjoying swimming, and floating on my back, feeling the hypnotic rocking soothe my entire being. And Mr. B and the Austrians would shoot by, riding the crest of some wonderful big wave. I longed to join them, but fear kept me near the shore.

On the fourth day of our holiday, Mr. B and I headed out for the first swim of the day. The Austrians were already far out in the water, silhouetted against the radiant horizon. I complained that I just couldn't get out far enough to ride a wave back to shore. The waves were too high—they tumbled me around like pieces of seaweed. Mr. B almost laughed. But he didn't. He gave me a wet, salty embrace.

"Come on," he said, waving me in. "I'll show you how to catch a ride."

"Here's the problem. You're trying to jump *over* the waves. Don't do that. Dive *through* the waves." He smiled. He was serious. I was supposed to dive through those fierce-looking tunnels of high-velocity sudden death. As I watched, he turned to face the next glistening bottle-green tube of water, and exactly as if he were diving off a board into a swimming pool, he plunged straight into the middle of the wave. As the wave smoothed out, there he was on the other side, waving at me. "See? That's all you have to do."

I was terrified. There was no way I was going to allow my feet to lose contact with the ocean floor, no way I would throw my body into the oncoming column of fast-moving water. It meant abandoning everything that seemed reasonable. Yet I trusted Mr. B. So I had to trust what Mr. B had told me. I knew he

wouldn't lie to me, and in fact, I'd watched him do—and survive—
the very thing he was urging me to do.

I asked myself to let go. My body, after a long pause, agreed.
I swam out with Mr. B to the place where the waves lay in waiting. The Austrians were watching, waving their encouragement.
I turned and faced the oncoming coil of water. I positioned my
body as I had seen them do. I aimed my arms toward the center
of the oncoming wave as it grew and rose into a towering adver-
sary. Then Mr. B shouted, "Now! Dive!" Forcing my feet to let go,
I shot into the middle of the wave, hitting it right at the center
of its curve.

I was suspended for what seemed like minutes. There, in
the middle of the rolling monster, was an utter stillness—no
noise, no turbulence, no rushing roar of danger. Just glass of
the most translucent palest green, glowing with the sunlight
visible through the thin membrane of water. And, then, whoosh!
I popped out the other side of the wave, into the silken calm
beyond the surf. Now I knew how it was done, and when the
next good wave arrived, I too jumped up and felt the water lift
me up and shoot me like a bullet straight toward land. I was in
a chute being hurled along, speeding through the water. The
sandy beach nudging against my hands and shoulders brought
me to a sudden stop.

Mr. B beamed and congratulated me on a spectacular ride.
The Austrians applauded and waved. I was exhausted but trium-
phant. In a million years I wouldn't have dared to do it, and yet I
had. Now that sense of trust and surrender, the letting go of fear
and diving through the wave, was inside of me forever.

your turn

Ever wondered whether you could ford a stream, climb a steep rocky cliff, or swim a mile? Try it. You will know yourself even better once you get to the other side.

54

Flying with My Father

My dad liked to fly on the weekends, at a small airstrip a few miles from where we lived. I'd seen him getting ready to go flying, like a kid with a flushed face, grinning at my mother and her worried expression of semi-disapproval. He was at home high up in the air, with only a thin membrane of fiberglass, wood, and aluminum between him and the invisible atmosphere of our lovely planet. He had flown planes as a teenager, then again as a pilot in the Air Force. After that, he designed planes. The carport of our house in the Virginia suburbs always housed a half-built experimental airplane, rather than an automobile.

When I was twelve, he asked me if I wanted to go flying with him. Of course, I said yes. I'd never gone flying with my dad, just the two of us. The plane was quite small, a two-seater with the pilot in front, passenger right behind. As narrow as a human body. One propeller on the nose of the plane. I jumped up onto the wing and slipped inside. With my dad as the pilot, I had no fear.

Until we took off. Then the shaking and noise of the small craft provided a reality check. We were aiming high up, up into the sky. The land below dropped rapidly away, roads, cars, houses, and trees all growing smaller and smaller. The clouds came up close for a look. Sun glinted off the Potomac River. I saw the Washington Monument. Excitement quickly took the place of fear. This was glorious. I was high up in the sky in a small plane sharing the same sort of excitement that had branded my father early in his life. No wonder he loved it.

"Do you want to take the stick?" my father asked. He meant, did I want to steer the plane with the simple rudder in the center of the floor. Yes, I did. I held onto the steering mechanism for all I was worth. "Hold it straight," he told me. And then he said, "Let's aim to the left." And so I did, and the plane ever so gently rolled to the left, sweeping new views up toward our eyes as it did.

273

"Let's go a bit higher," he said, "just pull back on the stick." I pulled back, and the plane began to climb upward. I was thrilled. What a moment, discovering how it was possible to be transported up into the sky, high above the firm support of the land, into an invisible kingdom where the clouds lived.

All of a sudden, the sound stopped. I could hear nothing but silence. We were a thousand feet off the ground in a tiny capsule of silence. The engine had stopped. No power. Just free floating. "Daddy," I wailed. "What's going on? There's no power."

My father took over the stick. He was chuckling. "I stalled the engine," he explained. He had deliberately slowed down enough for the engine to quit, then magically restarted it again. My entire body slumped with relief. I could feel my chest pounding with excitement.

"Okay," my dad shouted over the noise of the engine. "Let's do a somersault." I held on tight and watched the earth turn slowly to the right and keep on turning until the sky and the earth were all back in place again. My body memorized that sensation, the slow, continuous, 360-degree rolling circle. That rare sensation was locked into me. I have loved being high in the sky, in any kind of airplane, or hang glider, since that time flying with my father. I also learned that I had the choice to respond to uncertain situations, even dangerous ones, with a kind of courage that is founded on part trust and part spirit of adventure.

I'm not sure I thanked my dad for sharing something so priceless with me. But he could tell by my flushed cheeks and bright eyes as I told the story to my mother that night. Not only did I get to know him in a new way, he had given me a rare experience. In restarting that engine, he had started up something inside of me. He couldn't have known how much I would take to that movement, that exhilaration, the sensation of flying and being mobile and agile high up in the sky. But I'd like to think he suspected I would love it.

274

your
turn

Take stock of the defining moments in your life. They can be traumatic, joyful, or wildly improbable, but they are always unforgettable. Trace yourself back to those moments. What difference have they made in your life?

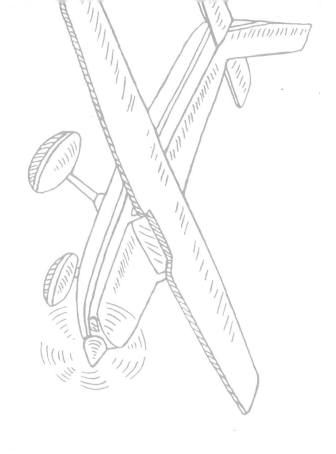

55

Time Sharing

The hummingbird was staring straight at me through the dining room window, darting and swooping around the empty feeder hanging from a hook under the eaves.

"I can't feed you now," I wailed at the tiny creature. My hands were full of dishes and the table was still messy with dinner plates. I asked myself: What would Nat do?

I had met Natalie singing with the concert choir. We were both in the alto section and started standing next to each other, helping each other with music notation and pronunciation of old Latin. She often came to rehearsal with her hair still wet from the shower, wearing too-tight sweaters and sensible shoes. She rarely smiled when she was concentrating on the music and she always bore her rounded body with a proud stance. This woman was not in the least uptight about how she looked or what she cared most about. Just standing next to her made me feel good. "Come over any time," Natalie told me after music rehearsal. "We can practice our music together."

Turns out she meant it. After making sure she was home, I did stop by one afternoon. It was a few weeks before Christmas, our concert was getting close, and, as she opened the door, I was greeted by the barking of two dogs and the blissful aroma of pumpkin pie baking in the oven. "I'm practicing up for our big holiday dinner," she explained. "Come in, I'll make tea."

Where were we going to sit? I wondered, looking around at the cluttered living room. Every surface showed evidence of some craft project or another. A huge Christmas tree occupied one corner of the small bungalow. A coffee table was laden with wrapping paper, pieces of quilting, and a laptop computer. An open scrapbook laid on the kitchen table next to several piles of old photographs; obviously Nat had been engaged in a project when I came to the door. But I moved the dogs aside, squeezed past the old upright piano (a family heirloom Natalie adores), and made it to the kitchen table, where Nat was already setting out her mother's china teacups and a small plate of cookies.

"I know, Christina, you're going to protest that you can't stay, that you're busy. I know you are. But I know you can have a cup of tea." Nat smiled a smile that amplified each of her beautiful features. It was a beautiful and persuasive smile. Why *was* I always in a rush? She had been in the middle of a photo project, with pie in the oven, but she didn't seem rushed or even annoyed by my visit. She was calm, completely in the moment, happy to be sitting here with me having a cup of tea. I was in the presence of a rare creature, a woman who was never too busy to take time for a friend.

A few more visits taught me that there's always a pot of soup or stew simmering on the stove at Nat's house. She makes her own tablecloths, knits mittens for her nieces and nephews, loves to please her husband with his favorite foods, and volunteers at hospitals and nursing homes, singing show tunes, folk music, and Christmas carols. No wonder she has so little time for housework.

How can she live with this level of chaos? I wouldn't be able to cope with the messy projects everywhere, every surface colonized by books, sewing, paperwork, and bits of yarn. I know I would go nuts dealing with the barking dogs who insist on parking themselves directly underfoot. Yet Nat talks to her old dogs with love in her voice, urging them to "go visit another room," with no hint of impatience in her voice. And how could I possibly just drop what I was doing when someone came to visit, drop everything and make them tea, invite them to sit down for a while, just to visit, just to be together?

After meeting Nat, how could I not?

Nat makes every day count. She has simply let go of some of life's mundane domestic tasks, doesn't obsess about her physical appearance, and allows herself the time and space to enjoy her friends, her family, and her projects. She isn't about to put off until *someday* what is right in front of her. You can see why she makes people feel good.

We sat at the piano together that day and worked on the alto parts, laughing, hitting wrong notes, and occasionally triumphing. I left her house with a smile on my face, having shed the tension I felt when I arrived, and thinking that maybe, just maybe, I could bypass the after-dinner crumbs and attend to the hummingbirds.

So next time, I did what Nat would do. I stopped fussing with the table and went to refill the hummingbird feeder. I love watching the tiny iridescent birds, hovering and whirring down to drink up the nectar. Their beauty is a momentary gift. The crumbs can always wait.

56

Painting
the Rock

Friends of the Spanish painter Antonio Lopez Garcia asked him why it had taken so many years to finish a painting of a quince tree in his orchard. He finally confessed that the whole point was just to be near the tree.

My sweetheart Jack invited me to join him one morning to go landscape painting a few miles up the coast. He equipped me with a portable easel, a canvas, a few brushes, and oil paints. We drove to our destination, gathered our gear in canvas tote bags, and trekked out to a flat spot overlooking the waves. There in front of us, jutting up out of the tide was a rock that had been sculpted by wind and waves into a colossal pyramid that reflected the swirling green of the waves and gleamed gold in the sun. A magnificent rock, filled with cracks and seams and topped with stubborn, hardy lichens and a few insistent seagulls.

With Jack's help I set up the easel and got my small canvas set in place. He offered me some of his brushes and paints. On a small wax paper palette, I squeezed out some blue, green, a red for mixing into purple, burnt sienna, and white. Grabbing a few brushes and some rags made from torn sweatshirts, I gazed at the rock poised like a jewel in its marine setting, and started sketching with a piece of brown conté crayon. It didn't look too bad, a bit lopsided perhaps, but I soon grew impatient and started applying paint.

Looking at the rock—actually staring at the rock—I began to fill in some of the main features, concentrating on its heroic profile, and then filling in the bottom cracks and holes made by constant wave bombardment. My eyes moved back and forth, from the rock to the canvas, as lovers do attempting to memorize each other's faces. With each brushstroke I looked up to check. My eye and hand were rebuilding the rock and its surrounding ocean and sky. Back and forth, looking and painting, I struggled to make the painted rock look like it was actually made of a different substance than the water below and around it.

So this was what Monet had to contend with, I grumbled to myself, as the purple shadow on the left of the rock slowly changed into a soft gray-green, and then as the sun pushed through the fog, turned to a brilliant sandstone yellow. So many changes it was impossible to keep up. I cursed the rock's metamorphosis even as I began to fall under its spell.

"You have to work quickly," Jack reminded me, without lifting his brush from his own canvas. "Not only work quickly, but *look* quickly."

I had to learn to see with my entire body, not simply with my eyes. I needed to merge with the rock and discover its secret structure, the one that lay beyond (or perhaps inside) its outward appearance.

After about an hour, we were both tiring and losing our focus. Jack had finished a dynamic, impressionistic portrait of the rock looking firm and heroic, while I had captured the rock somewhere between sea and sky and somewhere between statuesque and sketchy. It was a start. More than that—it was compelling. I wanted more of this.

The following weekend we went out to the same cliff, overlooking the same rock. Even without an easel and paintbrush, coming to this spot would have been a sensual joy. Light sparkled on the waves and the tall grasses were aromatic in the early morning air. Rabbits popped out of the nearby trail flashing their white tails. A red-tailed hawk observed us from a distant telephone pole. The surf purred and roiled, punctuating the morning mist with damp thunder as the tides came and went below our cliffside perch. When the fog came in close, temporarily thickening the morning sunlight, we were enclosed inside an opalescent cocoon of soft pastel hues.

284   It didn't take long for me to grasp that the act of painting was an excuse—the important thing was to be there, to let the place, the subject, the world in all of its sensory abundance, sink in. Every time I see that same rock, I see it as an intimate part of my sensory experience. I understand that piece of the world through my whole body.

Painting outdoors was a chance for me to understand, to see the object of my gaze more intimately than I could ever have expected. Focusing my attention and working with the paint to capture the exact colors and forms of the rock, I started to know this place as a genuine acquaintance. It became familiar in a way that merely looking at it would never have attained. My ability to appreciate the object of my perception became forever transformed. The rock and I exchanged points of view. It was now inside me, and I inside it. The rock and I were united, not only during the hours I spent painting on the cliff, but forever after.

your
turn

Visit a favorite spot—a bench, forest, park, or river. Go there at different times of the day. What changes do you feel in different weather? When do you find it most appealing? Perhaps take a notebook and record your impressions. Sketch this spot. Talk to it. (Listen for the reply.)

57

Uncurated Keepsakes

Many of us have trouble parting with old clothes, toys, or games from childhood, papers from college, single gloves that have long since lost their mates, and empty perfume bottles still heady with scent. We keep them because they still transmit an aura of pleasure, or importance. Our eyes love to look at them. They haven't faded into generic oblivion. We refuse to part with them because they keep us whole. They are our history, kept close at hand, available to open up and touch once more.

I keep such objects in a drawer with no name, a drawer filled with oddities, like some old Victorian cabinet of curiosities. The long ago and far away, in time and in space, are all inside that drawer. Some items linger by pure accident, others by sheer tenacity. The drawer exudes an undeniable power even though its contents are not organized. It's a private place. I go there to reach in and touch the familiar shapes. So reassuring. They're still there. And so am I.

My drawer of uncurated keepsakes contains two much-used, but now out-of-date passports. Some French francs from the time before the euro. A handkerchief with a map of Wiesbaden, Germany, printed on its crisp, perpetually folded cotton square; my eyes immediately catch the name of the street where we lived. A silver filigree pin from Portugal that belonged to my sister.

A little jewel case nestles in one corner, containing a few rhinestone barrettes from when I had long hair and one large aquamarine bead from a necklace (long gone) that belonged to my great-grandmother. A tube of lipstick that no longer opens. A teal silk scarf Jack bought me in Florence. A sachet filled with lavender made by a girlfriend as a birthday present. Two or three unidentifiable rocks considered important enough to keep. A twisted, velvety wisteria pod from either last year or last decade. A silk rose that belonged to my aunt, which she wore pinned to a favorite sweater—I like to pick it up to feel its soft faded texture. There's a thin, elaborately tooled leather wallet my father bought in Morocco when I was a kid. No one has ever used it, but it's finely made so why get rid of it? And there's a plastic bracelet that used to glow in the dark. Now it doesn't. A pair of 3D movie glasses. Tickets from trips to Europe, the theater, and the opera. A tiny manicure case made of beautiful red leather that doesn't open. And a single cotton glove without a mate.

There's also a box of nine squares of rock salt, each a slightly different color due to the differing amounts of minerals in them, from a childhood tour of the salt mines under Salzburg, Austria. My mother, father, sister, and I had to put on industrial overalls and slide down a long chute into the mine, where we visited a dozen chambers dug into the glittering crystalline rock. There is no file cabinet with a drawer for cubes of forty-year-old salt memorabilia, so it sits in the unnamed, all-purpose, uncurated keepsakes drawer.

Do I really need to keep old theater tickets? Old recital programs? Brochures from a remote museum I will never visit again? A ribbon trim from something I absolutely cannot identify or remember? Why not? Even if they've become dislodged from their own stories, from their original owners or ancestry, they have gained a new life as residents of this drawer. They have taken on a different narrative as objects somehow, and probably for no particular reason, they are important to me. I treasure them enough not to toss them away. When I open that drawer and see them there, I am situated reliably in a place I can recognize as home. If they're all still here, so am I.

your turn

Open that drawer, the one you fear because it lacks all sense of order. Examine the contents, one by one, and consider what they have in common. Maybe nothing. Eliminate anything you don't like, want, or need. Put what's left back in the drawer. Be content living with at least one drawer that makes no sense.

58

Phone Calls, Smiles, and Coffee Dates

The phone rings. It's my mother. I feel all of my body's cells turn toward her voice like a satellite dish responding to a signal. Her voice contains her face, the house where she lives, and the chair in which she sits as we talk. The sound of her voice brings with it all of our years together, her being my mother, the most constant presence in my life since I entered life. The phone calls continue the link that seems to have no beginning in time. Our voices meet and embrace, they connect us until we can see each other in person. Through the phone calls (I'd like to say they are daily, but neither of us is that organized), we reinforce and enjoy our being together.

Jack has a standing Sunday phone date with his best friend, Harvey, who lives three thousand miles away. The phone call allows their voices to come together and cheat the three time zones that pretend to separate them. The phone keeps them joined through a conversation they began thirty years ago.

A long-distance phone call was once a luxury indulged on special occasions—I remember Christmas calls to my grandparents when we were two continents away. Now the mobile phone keeps us in such constant contact that the sound of another's voice or the sight of their peculiar texts is a daily, indeed hourly, phenomenon. No longer as rare, such contact is still a strand in the network that grows and breathes and binds us each to each. We enter the world of our friends and invite them into ours—"You'll never guess who I saw today!"—by maintaining this simple open channel. It is a way of greeting the other. A way of saying, "I'm thinking of you, just wanted you to know."

I'm standing in line at the farmers' market. I have my eye on a particularly luscious display of late-harvest tomatoes. A woman approaches to take a closer look at the produce. She brings with her a small child in a stroller. I look down and notice the baby. All of a sudden the child sees me and a huge grin spreads across his little round pink face. The smile is so incandescent that others look down to see what bit of magic joy has just occurred. They are as smitten as I am with the simple perfection of a child's smile. The kid grows bold with the power of his smile. His feet start bouncing. We are all now saturated with this radiance. The smile is irresistible and leaves each of us standing around the stroller beaming and we keep on beaming as we continue on through the morning.

That small moment of shared smiles—always unplanned, always welcomed—has reminded us each of our shared humanness. We know the power of being a baby, and the pure gift of an unrehearsed smile from a little stranger, who is of course not a stranger at all but a moment in the life of us all.

I remember being in Barstow one hot morning, walking to the car to continue the drive to Las Vegas on Route 66. Seated on a bench outside the motel office were three ancient men, one with a cane, another holding a cup of coffee. They looked up as I walked by. I smiled at them—a big, glowing, Marilyn Monroe smile. All three lit up and smiled back. One of them waved. Another called out, "Good morning there, young lady." A momentary love fest ensued. Smiles all around. It had cost me nothing, and I could see how happy it made them. I was the real winner, receiving three big grins for my single one. All because I smiled at three strangers. Strangers no more.

Once a month I meet my friend Lisa for coffee. It began as coffee, and grew to include something in the way of a pastry. I stop by her house at 10:00 a.m. on the first Wednesday of the month—it's negotiable, but rarely alters. She pops out the front door and we begin jabbering. As I drive out of her neighborhood I ask, "Where shall we go today?" We pick a likely coffeehouse or cafe, somewhere within a ten-minute drive. Once we'd tried every-thing within a five-mile radius, we settled on our favorite spot, a bakery that had plenty of parking, terrific coffee, untold diverse pastries, and always a table available for us to occupy.

Lisa is a fellow writer and so sometimes the monthly coffee date includes kvetching about how our work is (or isn't) coming along. We unravel literary snarls together. Other times there are pictures to share from some recent bit of travel. Mostly the point is to sit there and feel each other's familiar shape, smile, tone of voice, and laughter. The laugh is always a big piece of the joy we take in each other's company. Frankly, if anyone asked me, "So what do you and Lisa talk about?" I wouldn't be able to come up with a solid reply. What we do is meet over coffee and smile and listen and taste the pastries. I offer her a bite of mine if I think it's something she'd like. We never question why we need to get together. We simply accept that it should happen, so we make time for this time together.

Like the smile or the phone call, the meeting over coffee solidifies a longstanding friendship. It ensures that a bit of me is infused by our time together. Things are now seen through the renewed lens.

When things are humming along in the social world, we seep in and out of each other's pores. I smile at a stranger, and that smile is enough to open the door of the world a crack wider than it was before. The stranger catches the smile and throws it further. And now there are others who begin to smile. The attitude of uplift shared—a smile—changes all the alignments in the body. A smile is our inner, secret joy turned inside out, like the lining of a coat now worn on the outside for others to see.

When I was a very serious young woman, I was convinced that the whole point of meeting with someone was to solve some problem, talk something over, or plan a specific event. Now I know that being with another person, at its fullest, is simply about being with them. Being with Lisa, I am also with my self. I expand in moments like this, moments where there is no need of an agenda. The smile shared with a stranger has no quantifiable outcome. It serves no practical purpose. It is a moment of just being human. The priceless and mundane poetry of communication. The coffee is just the icing on the cake.

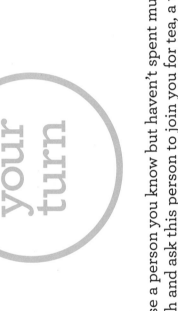

your
turn

Choose a person you know but haven't spent much time with and ask this person to join you for tea, a walk, bird-watching, or just hanging out over coffee. Give this encounter a chance to become something more. You'll know if it's not the right fit, and if not, you've still explored your openness to others. No harm done.

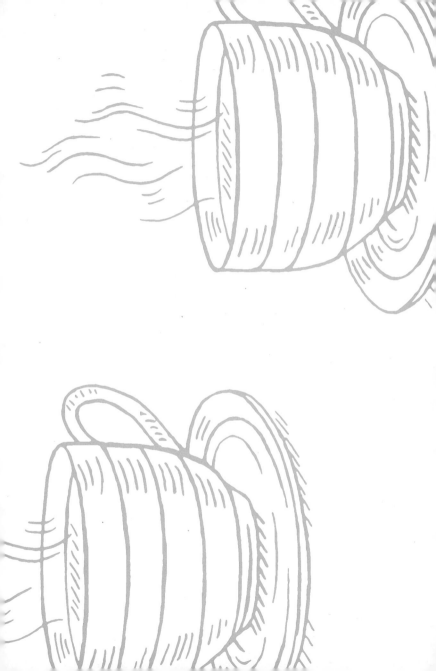

$$\left(59\right)$$

Visionaries

One cold, clear night, Jack and I dragged a mattress up to the roof of Irene's adobe near Joshua Tree and lay down under a dark night sky scattered with stars. Airplanes cruised overhead at regular intervals, their red lights pulsing. We spotted a satellite drifting slowly across the sky from right to left. Scorpio glittered, the Big Dipper sparkled, and even the usually veiled Pleiades pounced on our eyes from their celestial perch. The evening sky was anything but dark. It glowed and throbbed and twinkled with stars, planets, planes, and other technological lights.

When I turn off the lights at night in a heavily curtained bedroom I am plunged into a black envelope of space that is thick and tangible. But I've learned that it too contains much more than simple darkness. Inside this dark space I can hear a low hum (the sound of the earth turning?). Sounds from outside the room soon come into focus, each one leading somewhere, to some other person's life, or a car moving at a certain speed. I can detect aromas that seem connected to the darkness, and to memories—vividly shaped memories—that fill the darkness, as if my consciousness craves stimulation and in this darkened room, has decided to create its own.

The room is dark, but it isn't empty of sensation. It is full, fuller than it might have been with the lights on, because I just let go and listen, watch, smell, touch—I seek the sensory streams that are there, but which are usually obscured by the activities of the day.

In his 2004 documentary *The Eye of the Heart*, Bill Viola talks about being in his room at night as a kid and listening as the sounds of his parents getting into bed faded and the house grew still. Listening and watching the darkness itself, he hoped to catch a glimpse of things beneath the level of everyday perception. That quest led to the probing, even archetypal images he has created in his career, each of which refused the limits of ordinary sensory expectation. He pushes what he can see to images that are as far as he can see. Slowing down the film, he stays firmly fixed on a single human feature for longer than usual—he sees further.

Creative artists of all sorts share with me that expansion of everyday experience. Probing deeper into the concrete sensory world, composers, writers, and painters make work that amplifies the way we see, feel, and touch the everyday. I love the novels of Charles Dickens, particularly my favorite, *Great Expectations*. The characters Dickens created and the discoveries his imagination unearthed by way of their struggles and dramas have enlarged my experience of the world. Like the sensory richness of Viola's darkened space, Dickens's imagination invites me to expect more detail and nuance from human actions and longings.

There's a woman I sing with whom I used to watch and puzzle over as she engaged with the younger students in our rehearsals. I see her now through the Miss Havisham lens Dickens has given me. The woman's behavior has taken on a richer set of motives and probabilities. *Ah, she's attempting to transform the young people into her surrogates,* I think, watching her movements and gestures. Dickens's imagination has thrown light, color, and emotion on insights that might have remained hidden from me.

Virginia Woolf's genius uncovered a universe of robust experiences for me. Her masterpiece *To the Lighthouse* flooded me with sensory nuances. I was plunged deep into my own native language, now renewed and illuminated by comets and starbursts of fictional conversation. *So this is how language might work,* I realized, delighted to have new textures emerge from the most ordinary words and sentences. Woolf's imagined dinner table talk with its seeming non sequiturs of gossip, fearful interpretations, and dawning love heightened my own spoken word experience. From her imagination came my newly expanded awareness of ways that disarmingly applied words can force open my encounters with the world.

Every artist with a genuine vision does this. Bob Dylan's lyrics infuse my responses to a disappointment, or lost love. These everyday experiences become more than I thought them to be. Dylan's creativity has mined the unknown and produced illumination for even the slightest moments of my life. Like the art of Woolf and Dickens, Bob Dylan's music has inflected my everyday awareness with deeper sounds, sharper aromas, and more tender hues. I chose to live in a world richer in texture, sound, and images, something like Viola's expanded sensory expectations. Expecting more leads me into other corners of feeling alive.

302

your turn

Be still and allow your body to listen for sounds usually scrambled and obscured by the noise of daily life. Wait for the quietest moment of the day (or night) and then begin to listen. Keep listening until a world of exquisite smallness and delicacy begins to appear.

60

Grand Canyon Sunset

The sign pointed toward the Grand Canyon National Monument. Jerry, my college boyfriend, and I both suspected that the much-hyped scenic wonder was bound to be a disappointing cliché. Big and deep and vast: we could imagine all of that. But the car had a mind of its own and pretty soon we were approaching the South Rim.

We'd left New York right after graduation on a long, cross-country road trip and we had become enchanted by the southwest. The desert seemed to expand as we drove through it, stretching back in every direction until it was emptied of anything man-made and revealed its true mineral heart. Everything seemed to glow, including the giant tortoise we spotted, stopping the car and getting out because we wanted to touch its polished shell. We saw boulders the size of a VW van; the filigreed bone structure of ocotillo cacti, each thin branch topped by an orange flame.

At the South Rim, we parked the car, paid our entrance fee, and walked up the trail. Far in the distance a lightning storm was providing a fierce light show of percussion and fireworks. But the storm was remote from where we stood in the brilliant afternoon sun. The canyon walls glowed with colors that seemed alive, orange and gold and rich red, moving along the walls at different hues, paler where the sun hit, plunging into deep tones of purple and blue where the shadows had already begun to form.

The light changed rapidly in the late September afternoon. The sun illuminated the canyon rim while the crenellated strata, band upon band, descended into a darkness of at least three dimensions. The harsh rock turned into some deep velvet substance that spoke to our bodies. Our bodies and the canyon began an internal dialogue, exchanging color and mineral information. Our bodies and the rock walls seemed made of the same stuff. Our minds resisted comprehending. Our hearts bowed in wonder. 307

Jerry and I stood together, not speaking, barely touching, until the color had drained completely from the braid of minerals, desert flora, and cosmic dust. Once the sun had evaporated into a band of pink hovering high above the twilight, bold stars came down to explore the higher edges of the canyon. Or so it seemed, so indelible were the stars and planets that bloomed in the dry night air.

We were so overwhelmed with the hugeness, the splendor beyond comprehension, that instinctively we turned to each other and kissed. The kiss was an affirmation of the sight we were witnessing, our covenant with the place and its incomprehensible magic. The Grand Canyon had captured us in its geological web of time travel. It had swallowed us up and we remain within it to this day.

61

Fire in the Rain

The summer I was seventeen, my cousin Danny took me back-packing in the Cascades. Danny and I had been close friends since childhood. Two years older than I, he had stayed in the West, learning its canyons and trails, becoming an expert skier, mountain climber, and logger. I had jumped at his offer to trek through the rainforest of Washington state. Danny had promised me a true rainforest, a place of perpetual mists, lush with streams and waterfalls and unimaginable trees and plants, where over 150 inches of rain fell each year.

Everything glistened with moisture. We followed the trail when we could, along tiny streams bordered by thick quilts of moss and massive fallen tree trunks. Even when the trail disappeared, we pushed on, thanks to Danny's topo map. Three days into the forest, the sun broke through the high canopy—briefly—and brilliant light plunged down to the edge of the rivulet near our trail. I knelt down for a drink when a glittering strand of water droplets suspended in a spider's web caught my eye. A rainforest necklace of diamonds.

We hiked for a few miles each morning before stopping for a bite. When night fell, sleep came instantly. But now, on the fourth day, a light drizzle was rapidly turning into rain. A cold, tired, backpacking newbie, I must have been a pathetic sight. Danny took pity on me. Yes, he agreed with my unspoken wish:

we should probably set up camp early and wait out the rain and the growing chill. We pitched the tent under a sheltering spruce, a tree so huge its thick branches had created a spot where the rain wasn't too heavy. But staying warm was another thing.

"Come on, Teen," he cajoled in an irritatingly upbeat voice. "I'll show you how to make a fire."

I almost laughed. He had to be kidding. But he wasn't. Pointing to a nearby pine tree, he told me to start gathering needles.

"Look around," he commanded. "Try to find needles under the top layer, ones that aren't so damp."

Some fallen branches of pine looked feasible, and we started making a little collection. He took a handful of pine needles and a bunched-up piece of tissue paper, and put a match to the small mound, blowing on the needles as they started to glow. Nope, too damp. I was clapping my hands together to keep them warm and beginning to despair. Patience was never my first language. I was cold and we were in the middle of nowhere, even if it was a beautiful nowhere.

Danny persisted, raising his voice a bit as he urged me to get on the ball and bring more pine needles. "And some small sticks—just look around!" He started over with the match, a crumpled chocolate bar wrapper and the pine needles. Gently, he blew on the pine needles, carefully aiming the match, one after another, into what he hoped was the driest part of the tinder. Suddenly the little mound erupted into flame.

"Find more paper!" he said. I managed to scrounge up another tissue from my jacket pocket, and slowly I fed little twigs into the flame, then larger ones. The sight of the smoke curling up toward the towering trees was incredibly heartening. We grinned at each other.

An hour later, we were warm enough to boil some water for soup. It had been a long day and I was dead tired. But I had acquired something new and valuable. The ability to build a fire in the rain is a rare skill I'm proud of to this day.

your
turn

Ever push yourself past what you think you can endure?
Try something you are convinced you cannot achieve.
Run for a mile. Shoot an arrow straight into a bull's-eye.
Memorize a beautiful poem—in another language.

$$\left(\begin{array}{c}62\end{array}\right)$$

Glacier Rinse

After five days in the wilderness, I was dying to wash my hair. It was long, tangled, matted, and flecked with bugs, Spanish moss, and bits of mud from the trail. I was in the middle of a forest in the Cascade Mountains, not exactly the right moment for a wash and a blow dry. But I hated having dirty hair. On the day before our arrival at the river's edge—and our turnaround point for the trek—I knew I couldn't put off washing my hair any longer. Danny laughed much longer than necessary. He was going to enjoy the sight of his city cousin washing her long hair in the wilderness stream that skirted our campsite.

Without hot water, we had been washing our cooking pots in the swift-moving streams, scrubbing utensils with wild horsetail stalks. My hands had gotten used to managing without warm water. But the human head has much more tender demands. The stream was small enough for me to lower my head into without being swept away into oblivion. I lay down on my back and tilted my head backward. Just before my head touched the water, Danny shouted to me from the campsite, "By the way, that water comes from a glacier up the mountain!"

Something like an electrical current zapped through me as my head hit the icy stream. The cold knocked the breath out of me and it took all my willpower to keep from snapping my head back out and running back to camp. But the major shock had already happened. I might as well get on with it, I figured. I reached around, located the shampoo bottle, and managed a quick lather before dunking my head back into the frigid water to rinse. I emerged screaming. Danny threw a small towel in my direction and I dried off by the campfire. No campfire has ever felt so good—ever.

I left some of the city back there in the wild splendor of that forest, but even more of the forest came back with me to my real world. I brought it back in the form of moody weather, sensory beauty, aching feet, cold nights, and strong muscles. I felt physically toughened. I had acquired an expanded vocabulary of extreme sensations. My scalp can still feel the shock of that glacial water as if it just happened.

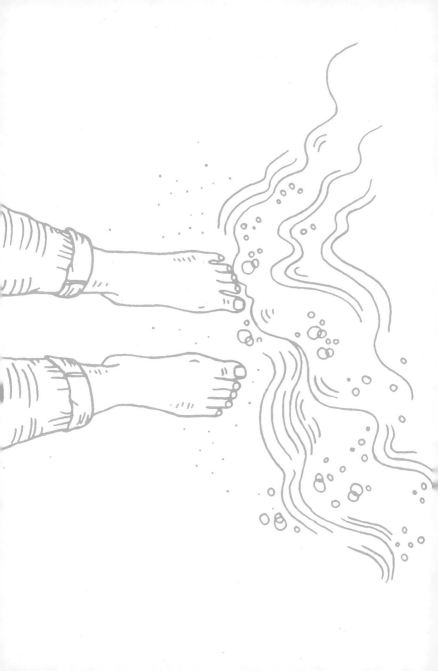

your turn

Find a way to step outside that warm and cozy zone, if only for an hour or an afternoon. Walk in the rain until you are completely soaked. Make a snowball with your bare hands. Take off your shoes and wade in the chilly ocean. What has your body learned?

63

Natural Disaster

At a party last winter, the weather was a hot topic of conversation. It had been raining for days, with no sign of letting up. One of my colleagues, Will, was standing near me regaling some friends about a storm he'd been caught in many years ago. He was driving home along the coast. A tree had fallen on someone's car, blocking the highway between San Francisco and Santa Cruz, so he had to drive all the way back north to Half Moon Bay, up over the mountains, and back down along another highway in order to get home.

"I'll never forget that storm," he concluded, shaking his head. "It took me an extra three hours to get home that night."

I remembered that storm, too. And I remembered that tree. That night, it had come crashing through my windshield and nearly killed me.

Will laughed in disbelief. "*You're* the one who got hit by the tree?"

Yes, I told him. I'm the one.

Jack and I were driving back down the coast from San Francisco and into a fast-moving storm. The radio warned of gale force winds. The sky moved in close, hugging the land. The trees lining the highway bent lower and lower, almost horizontal to the ground.

Why were we out in such treacherous weather? We'd simply hoped to rush home ahead of the wind and the rain. It was only an hour-and-a-half drive, and storm or no storm, we were anxious to get home. But the storm had other plans.

About forty minutes into our drive south down Highway One, the trees began moaning. I was driving Jack's little blue Honda Civic, which felt tiny and vulnerable in the corridor of tall, twisting cypresses and pines. Both Jack and I pretended we weren't scared out of our usually rational minds. To distract me, he started talking about the dinner we'd had the night before, at a new restaurant in San Francisco.

317

"I really liked that braised mushroom dish," he said. "What kind of mushrooms were those?"

"Porcinis and shiitakes," I said. I had loved that dish, too.

I peered through the windshield, barely able to see through the driving rain. I tried to focus on the reggae playing on the radio. Lilting and upbeat, it was an antidote to the turbulence outside.

"If anything happens, remember that I love you," I said, half teasing, half bravado.

I was hunched over the steering wheel, eyes glued to the road ahead. Jack smiled at me and reached over to touch my cheek. And high above, to my right, the tree started to fall. In an instant that felt like years, I turned the wheel away from the tree's trajectory—the passenger side of the car. I was told later that I blacked out. But I remember the sight of the huge tree, a seventy-five-foot Monterey pine, stretched across the hood of the Civic. The rest of my memories are fragments: Jack and I, sitting on the side of the road, holding hands. "You'll be fine," he kept telling me. The bloody scratch on Jack's forehead—"Hopefully it will leave a dramatic scar," he joked. The thick army surplus sweater I wore covered with blood; two men assuring me they had called for an ambulance. Then I was inside the ambulance, my head strapped to a gurney, and the paramedics were telling me not to move. Next to me sat Jack, still clutching my hand tightly. He never let go.

The tree had crashed through the windshield and hood of our car. One of its branches had jabbed my face, puncturing my left cheek. The paramedics couldn't believe my jaw wasn't broken. For some reason, all I could think was, *What am I going to tell my mother?* The huge tree blocked all traffic from the north, including the car driven by Will, the man at the party. Five weeks later, I started feeling a tingling in my right hand. I had an MRI, and then emergency surgery to remove a subdural hematoma.

But Jack and I survived. I am fine; we are fine. In the strange poetry of near-death, the experience created a bond between us that is uniquely and deeply ours. Each year on the anniversary of our encounter with the falling tree, we return to the exact spot where it happened. We leave early in the morning and drive back up the coast highway to what we flippantly call the "Corridor of Death." We take our coffee out to the pile of logs, all that remains of the huge pine. "There's our tree," we tell each other, excited by this annual ritual. One year Jack photographed me perched on the fallen arboreal villain. We raise our cups to the tree felled by the storm, and to each other for having been tested and having prevailed, and we renew our joy and good fortune in being alive together.

your turn

Have you had some life-threatening experience? Try finding a way to commemorate it, and to celebrate your bond with life.

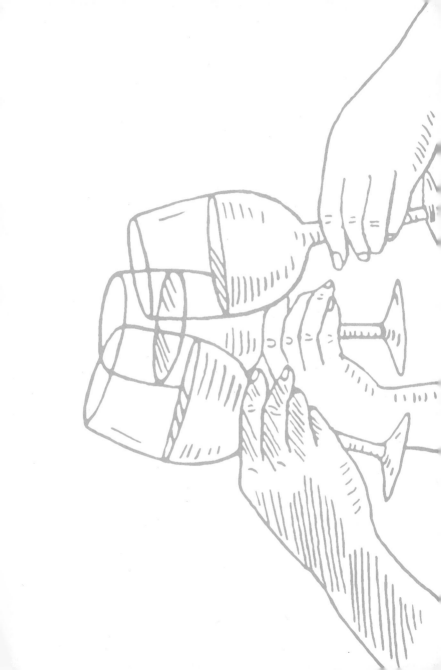

64

Hearing Green,
Touching Yellow

The path to discovering my home in the world became clearer the more I looked into the simplest moments of my everyday life. Expecting more, being attuned to each touch, encounter, and flavor, I found more. One key was in releasing the boundaries that keep our sensations carefully corralled. What if color can be connected with music? Or aroma deeply linked with imagery? Once I began rejecting the confinement of tight categories, the world—even the simplest ways of living in the world—blossomed into a profusion of sensory complexity and intimacy.

In Book IV of his epic exploration of memory, *In Search of Lost Time,* Proust describes his lover Albertine's laugh as "pungent, sensual, and revealing as the scent of geraniums." Even though he is clearly offering us a lyrical literary analogy—comparing her laughter to the aroma of flowers—his potent image suggests that the way we experience others is laced with unexpected sensory depths. To simply *hear* her laugh is to miss much that waits to be enjoyed.

When Tom Robbins wrote in *Jitterbug Perfume,* "the beet is the most intense of vegetables," he spun another poetic phrase, one that catches us by surprise and suggests to the reader that she hasn't really considered the full possibilities of experience.

Once I read that Robbins line I reconsidered my expectations of ordinary experience, looking for and listening to what I might have overlooked.

Writing about wine, I have struggled to locate exactly the right description or characteristic of certain wines. Instead of remaining in the expected vocabularies of tart, dry, sweet, and tannic, I reached further and found deeper sensory qualities such as hints of terra cotta and orange peel in sauvignon blanc. Clove and bay leaf, granite and tobacco are distinct flavor and aroma notes of a pinot noir I sampled recently. Once I began looking in larger domains of flavor and perfume, the wines I experienced took on increased depth, complexity, and above all, enjoyment.

That same attitude, in which I experience porous boundaries of sensation and experience, can be applied to almost every tangible aspect of life.

Here's another example. The Chilean poet Pablo Neruda wrote these lines in his love sonnets about his beloved's hands: *When I die, I want your hands upon my eyes/I want the light and the wheat of your beloved hands/to pass their freshness over me one more time.*

I could consider hands of light and wheat to be simply the product of poetic license, words chosen by a poet to amplify the power of his image. But what if I apply poetic images—hands made of light and wheat—to the quality of everyday experience? How much richer and more exciting might each day become? My own hands *can* become like small children, wayward and impatient. Or the red-winged blackbirds outside my office create sonic architecture of gold filigree and rust. I don't mean adding on some adjectival adornment to an everyday moment or object, but actually deepening that moment or object by expecting a transformative braiding of sensations.

My dear Jack brings an unmistakable feeling of yellow light with him wherever he goes. When I touch his neck and face I am filled with that yellow light, a living awareness of his uniqueness

323

that enters and saturates me. For me, the sound of a guitar is infused with the perfume of cognac and the bottle green of the ocean opens into swirling aromas of salt and sage. Van Morrison's voice is the color of bronze. Because I lean into these experiences, looking deep into them, I am able to find more sensory dimensions within them.

My each day swells with more nuance and energy when I allow color, for example, the freedom to be deeper, larger, than simply information on my retina. Red that creates excitement beyond the visual awaits only a mindful attitude to be experienced. The same is possible for all sensuous experience. Each bit of sensory information—what we see, the nuanced sounds we hear, texture, music, moonlight, garlic, sandpaper, my sister's name—can become portals leading in rich sensory directions.

The loose ends of my day, and my life, begin to converge as my senses—no longer simply individual strands of information—begin to entwine and collaborate. I can see the aroma of bay, smell the clouds and the ocean, hear the breathing of the reeds on the pond. My increasing experience of sensory intertwining parallels my awareness of how my sense of home is achieved—through the communion of adventure, texture, and experience.

Experience can be much more full, detailed, and creative than we assume it to be. The point isn't to force oneself into extreme, physically challenging experiences, but to open to full sensitivity, so that the richness of each experience isn't lost or neglected in favor of pushing on, pushing ahead, pushing beyond the present. I am fully alive when I'm willing to expect more from every detail of the day. All sensory encounters, however small and seemingly inconsequential, can carry profound insights.

Inside the flame the senses intermingle, spinning a web of all-encompassing fierceness—of heat, music, starlight, and spice. The senses embrace each other at every moment, sometimes more forcefully and clearly than at others. If I wish to separate them out for purposes of some project or exercise of course that can be done. But allowing the senses free rein to collaborate, embrace, and become something more complex and exciting—that we can also do. Being fully alive, I've discovered, means asking questions. Always. Being fully alive means listening for the answer. Yes is always the answer.

your turn

Can you hear the color blue? How do clouds taste? What aroma do you most associate with your childhood? Find an essential oil that appeals to you. Let its aroma enter your space. What's occurring between your body and the aroma?

65

Brahms
in London

My trip to London had a very specific goal. I had been lucky enough to score tickets for a performance of *Hamlet* starring a renowned actor. The opportunity was special enough to justify the long journey, and after a week in the English countryside, I settled into a rented flat across from Trafalgar Square. I'd purchased the sought-after tickets nearly a year ago and spent months anticipating the trip and the performance. Now that the long-awaited date with *Hamlet* was drawing near, I felt restless. Out on a morning walk I noticed the flyer on the door of St. Martin-in-the-Fields, the crisp white Christopher Wren church located at the northeast corner of Trafalgar Square. The flyer announced a free lunchtime concert of music by Bach and Brahms. Great music performed in the early eighteenth-century Anglican landmark? How could I pass this up?

A crowd filled the interior by the time I got there. I managed to find a seat on one of the raised side pews, sharing it with a young Czech man, two women from China, and a worn but dignified man of the streets. The diverse audience of young and old, visitors and residents was clearly energized, and there was generous applause when the performer came out with her cello.

At the first note the room became hushed. The young Korean

cellist began the opening of a Bach fugue, her bow coaxing sounds that felt like living creatures, singing and sighing from her instrument. The antique baroque music sparkled, and her interpretation took us directly to the mind of its creator. A single instrument swelling, aching, descending deep into the lowest reaches of the musical line. Like a slow sip of aged cognac. And then it was finished. The last note resonated for what felt like an eternity. We sat for a moment absorbing the gift she had offered. Then energetic applause, enough to invite several curtain calls.

Soon began the main piece of the concert, a Brahms cello sonata, four movements expanding into the glowing rich panoramas of Brahms's mature period from a very brisk opening, into a long, slow adagio that felt like the autumnal colors of twilight. The music seeped into me and began to pry me open. I was defenseless against the sweep of sound and the brilliance of the performers. At some point, maybe halfway through the piece, I realized I was in tears.

At this moment, in this place, two young women had gathered up the great musical passion of Brahms and set it ablaze. They had swept me inside the flame and I was burning, weeping, complete. What had happened to me? Was it simply the expertise of the young musicians overwhelming my emotions? Partly. Was I swept away by recollections of making music in my own life? Yes. But it was a physical epiphany. As I listened to the last moments of Brahms, the cello and piano moving across each other's tonal dynamics and closing in on a fiery transcendent finish, I realized that nothing else reached into me like music.

This was why I had come so far to be here. It wasn't to see *Hamlet*. It was to reaffirm in one indelible moment how richly music has illuminated my life. Staying open to the unanticipated, I was given a moment of unexpected clarity and insight. How easily I might have missed it. Looking for *Hamlet* in London, I almost missed Brahms.

And the end of all our exploring
Will be to arrive where we started
And know the place for the first time.
— T. S. Eliot, "Little Gidding," *Four Quartets*

66

Homecoming

We call our resident scrub jay, "Bird." Not very original, but that's his name. Bird lands on the chair on our deck in a certain confident way. He announces by his unique body language that he is here. Here to be fed. We respond with a peanut, which he takes directly from our hands. Then he flies off toward the quarry, to a tree on the far side of the pond.

If we are momentarily oblivious to Bird's presence, he coolly approaches the glass sliding door, close to where Jack sits inside at the breakfast table. Bird then proceeds either to squawk or tap his beak against the glass. (Sometimes both.) We are charmed. We drop everything and get him a peanut. He is already perched on his chair by the time we slide open the glass door. Using his beak as a precision instrument, he grabs the peanut and flies off to his hideaway across the pond. Bird has been visiting our house, and accepting our offers of peanuts, for six seasons.

Coming downstairs to breakfast each morning I pass the *milagros* on the stairwell, the little silver medals Jack and I bought on a trip to Santa Fe. *That sideboard needs dusting again,* my eyes tell me. *How glad I am that I found this beautiful rug,* my feet tell me as I pad across the deep red carpet bordered with indigo diamond shapes. Jack has already prepared our favorite breakfast, soft-boiled eggs placed into the blue painted eggcups I bought years ago at a monastery shop in Tuscany. Black Assam tea is steeping in the pea green teapot. The toast is ready to take out of the toaster—today it will be a fragrant sourdough dotted with cranberries and walnuts. Even if I request oatmeal, Jack's default breakfast is soft-boiled eggs, so he usually goes ahead and makes us each an egg, which we consume while the hummingbirds outside our window keep us company.

Later, I cross the backyard and walk down the hill toward the pond, listening to my neighbor compulsively washing his car. He does this once a week. It is his ritual. The neighbor's new cat, Dino, has already been out prowling the well-worn animal trail that threads across our slender back fence. All the animals use that route—bobcats, feral cats, deer, coyotes, raccoons. The perfume of their many crossings incites Dino's daily stalkings; we see his black-and-white shape crouched into low-slung invisibility.

Bird's wife, Mrs. Bird, returns each winter. Right now we suspect she is with egg. She comes close to the glass door of the deck, but then flies up to a branch to wait. We toss a peanut out to her. Only after the glass door slides shut does Mrs. Bird swoop down to collect her peanut. Then she flies back up to the branch to get her bearings. Mrs. Bird is an entirely different creature from her mate.

Watching them day after day, year after year, I no longer see "birds," but have become engaged with individual birds. I have learned about them from watching the way they perch, their unique approaches to a treat. I have watched their flight paths from my hand offering the peanut to the willow trees across the pond where they have their secret homes. Certain individual birds make distinctive calls and songs.

Still, the variations of plants, weather, and animals repeat themselves in graceful fugues. I admire a trio of deer, a watchful mother and her two graceful fawns as they sail effortlessly over fences and hedges. A nesting pair of red-tailed hawks ride the

332

air currents in ascending spirals until they arrive at the rendez-vous point, back together on the same high branch of a cypress on the ridge. Gray squirrels fling themselves through the tree-tops to rob the jays of their hidden peanuts. Raccoons play and fight after sundown. Bats punctuate the deep turquoise of twi-light while owls softly pierce the night with their throaty call and response. Back and forth they speak to each other at 4 am.

Autumn's morning light seeps into the pond and quarry cliffs outside my window in ever-widening bands of orange. The orange is a new seasonal phenomenon; it's not there in sum-mer. The deepening colors of morning, the long indigo shad-ows invite me to consider the familiar landscape in a whole new mood. As the shadows lengthen so do the evenings—dawn gets lazier and morning comes while it's still dark out. There's a chill in the air that wasn't here a few weeks ago. Tuning in carefully I listen to the leaves rustling in the trees. What do they say? They sound dry, like bits of dried parchment or cellophane. They're no longer plump with moisture. I can actually hear autumn materializing. Dryness has made the leaves sound scratchy, more metallic, their mineral composition revealed as moisture wanes. Growing lighter, they are ready to release themselves from their branches.

The rise and fall, the spiraling of the seasons, departure and return: I am part of it all. The repeated rhythms are tangible, and I feel them in my body. The eyes see more than they are looking at; the hands feel beyond mere touch. Aromas scent us with place, the here as well as the then. The past lives on in our bodies, where it is always *right now*, always this moment and not a minute more.

"Perhaps home is not a place but simply an irrevocable condi-tion," James Baldwin suggested in *Giovanni's Room.* If he's right, I have to consider that other people have naturally grown into that condition, or were born with it, while I remained outside for so long. My irrevocable condition has been one of staying open to what unfolds in front of me, asking questions, being inquisitive. The home I longed for was less a condition than a transformation.

For me, home has become a chance finally to be in one place and to feel my connection to that place tighten and become intimate. I observe the Japanese maple in front, the way its color changes in autumn, its bare vulnerability in winter. I see the same coots in the pond fight their way joyfully into spring. I nurse the tangled nasturtiums through the rainy season—together (me fussing, they cooperating) we scoff at the idea that they are annuals and must be confined only to one lifespan.

My body tells me my place in the world. Home is something I can see, hear, feel in my body, especially my body as the bearer of repeated communion with the same place—the place, the seasons, the animals, the clouds endlessly varied, endlessly the same.

Once you've tasted a wonderful wine, a fully ripe tomato, a piece of dark chocolate, your body is forever tuned in a new and different way. The body acquires new intelligence, new confidence with this new knowledge. How our hands move reflects that mountain over there, or the car pulling up beside mine at a stoplight. These are the sensations that have called for my close attention and rewarded my attention by filling me with a sense of myself.

I agree with the author Don DeLillo, as he wrote in *Underworld,* that home is where you are most familiar to yourself. In my case, homecoming has also been an achievement, an active agreement between the universe and me that I will accept this moment; I will act upon this unexpected opportunity. Without action, there is no discovery, and without discovery, awareness remains shut tight. For me, seeking to live a life of heightened awareness has led to achieving a home in the world.

Once I stopped looking outward and stayed put, things changed. Home became the product of all of my physical actions, makings, tastings, and darings, and the weaving together of my joys with the person I love. Everything is deepened when we share our lives with others, or with one special other. Home is lying in bed at dawn next to Jack, feeling the warm shape of the bed around our bodies. Home is opening my keepsakes drawer to touch my beloved memory objects, or sitting at my desk and gazing out my window at the pond. Home is singing Mozart with my choir, meeting my friend Lisa for coffee, or smiling at a stranger on the street. These experiences and objects make up the unique shape of my home—my home in the world—and it is far more than a building with walls and a roof. Home is my arrival at a wide plain of acceptance and gratitude. Home is the self I have created, surrounded by the place that is mine. It is, simply, where I always am.

acknowledgments

To my sharp-eyed editor, Tai Moses, goes incalculable gratitude not only for helping to shape my ideas into sharper focus, but for nudging me toward the writing of this book in the first place. Bunnies forever Tai!

Thanks to Faye Crosby for her generous support, as well as to Cowell College at the University of California Santa Cruz.

I want to acknowledge the counsel, companionship, and intellectual savvy of some remarkable people who have journeyed with me. To those special ones who sparked and shared the adventure along the way—Jerry Kleiner, Daniel Gouin, Den Wilson, Alistair Moles, and Buz Bezore. Academic role model, Marjorie Grene; phenomenologists David and Jocelyn Hoy; karmic lightning rod, Rita Bottoms; coffee companion, fellow filmie, and advance party on the trail of literary endeavor, Lisa Jensen; sharp-eyed poet, journalist, and editor, Stephen Kessler; guru of cinematic analysis and sister in enlightened partying, Vivian Sobchack; discoverer, photographer, and affectionate encourager of my abilities, Keith Muscutt; loquacious visionary Ralph Abraham; partner in opera, coastal walks, and cafe society, Angela Beck; shamanic maestro and musical inspiration, Nathaniel Berman; and sage, counselor, and beloved thorn in my side, Laurel Holloway.

To my mother, Marie, goes my love and all the credit for igniting my unquenchable curiosity about this improbable voyage called Life, and to my father, Don, undying thanks for his gift of maps, travel, and all those many, life-changing Sunday drives.

Finally, deepest gratitude to my beloved Frank Galuszka—partner of my life's adventures and daily mysteries—and all the dreams to come. With him, I live most joyfully inside the flame.

—Christina Waters

about the author

Christina Waters is a fifth generation Santa Cruz native, raised all over the world (thanks to an Air Force dad), with an academic background and real world training in journalism, painting, music, woodworking, hang gliding, trail running, reiki, organic gardening, and teaching.

Waters grew up in France, Germany, and northern Virginia with many summers spent in California. She received a BA in Anthropology from George Washington University in Washington, DC and went on to write her dissertation on Jean-Paul Sartre's theory of the imagination, to earn a PhD in Philosophy from the University of California, Davis.

An accomplished musician, Waters performs with the UCSC Concert Choir and regularly exhibits her expressionist oil portraits in local galleries. She teaches in the Arts at UC Santa Cruz and writes for publications in the Bay Area and Santa Cruz, where she lives with painter Frank Galuszka.

about the illustrator

Alice Koswara is a graphic designer, illustrator, and painter. She was born and raised in Jakarta, Indonesia and currently lives in San Francisco with her husband Eric Broers and their two cats.

related titles from
parallax press

Awakening Joy, James Baraz and Shoshana Alexander

Happiness, Thich Nhat Hanh

The Mindful Athlete, George Mumford

Mindfulness in the Garden, Zachiah Murray

Not Quite Nirvana, Rachel Neumann

Small Bites, Annabelle Zinser

Ten Breaths to Happiness, Glen Schneider

World as Lover, World as Self, Joanna Macy

Zooburbia, Tai Moses

PARALLAX
PRESS

Parallax Press is a nonprofit publisher, founded and
inspired by Zen Master Thich Nhat Hanh. We publish books
on mindfulness in daily life and are committed to making
these teachings accessible to everyone and preserving them
for future generations. We do this work to alleviate suffering
and contribute to a more just and joyful world.

For a copy of the catalog, please contact:

Parallax Press
P.O. Box 7355
Berkeley, CA 94707
parallax.org